Heroes of Peace

A History of the Third Kentucky Infantry
in the Spanish-American War

Colonel Greg Eanes, USAF (Ret)

Cover Photo:

Members of the Eighth Massachusetts Infantry in a skirmish line. They were brigaded with the Third Kentucky Infantry at the San Severino Castle in Matanzas City, Cuba. *(Papers of William Thomas Taylor, Co. A, Third Kentucky Infantry)*

Copyright © 2016 Greg Eanes
Published by The Eanes Group, LLC
Crewe, Virginia
Manufactured in the United States of America
All rights reserved

Virginia Certified SDVOSB and Microbusiness
SWAM No. 709249

Eastern National Bookstore Vendor #1934

ISBN: 1530755344
ISBN-13: 978-1530755349

DEDICATION

To Nancy, Jo Ann and
the men of the Third Kentucky Infantry

CONTENTS

	Acknowledgments	i
1	Lexington, Kentucky	1
2	Camp Thomas	15
3	The 'Battle' of Lexington	29
4	On To Cuba!	69
5	Occupation Duty	79
6	Battalion Posts	97
7	Demobilization and Home	119
8	Annex 1-Chronology of the Spanish-American War and the Third Kentucky	133
9	Annex 2-Division and Brigade Assignments	141
10	Annex 3-Regimenal Roster	143

ACKNOWLEDGMENTS

This work would not have been written had it not been for Mrs. Nancy Single and her sister Jo Ann whose grandfather, Private William Thomas Taylor, was a member of Company A, Third Kentucky Infantry, U.S. Volunteers. Mrs. Single contacted me, as a member of the Sons of Spanish-American War Veterans, regarding the proper disposition of her grandfather's papers which included letters from the period, numerous photographs and other mementos. We published these as <u>The Papers of William Thomas Taylor</u>, edited with explanatory notes and other comments. In doing the background research on Private Taylor's unit and its activities I came across more information than was appropriate to include in that volume and determined to write a separate regimental history. This is that history. It would not have been written had Nancy not reached out to try to preserve her family's military history.

CHAPTER 1

LEXINGTON, KENTUCKY

After several years of tensions resulting from the Cuban war for independence, the sinking of the *USS MAINE* in Havana Harbor on February 15, 1898 provided the spark that lit the fuse of war between Spain and the United States. A U.S. Navy investigation determined the ship was sunk by external source such as a mine while a Spanish investigation determined the ship was sunk by an internal explosion.

In response to mounting public and Congressional pressure, President William McKinley asked Congress on April 11 for authority to use armed military force to end the suffering of the Cuban people and threats to American economic interests. Congress authorized war on April 19 and passed the Volunteer Army Act on April 22nd. On April 23rd the President issued a national call for 125,000 volunteers to serve in an army to fight in Cuba. Spain declared war the same day. McKinley issued an additional 75,000 volunteers on April 25th.

The Third Kentucky U.S. Volunteer Infantry was one of four Kentucky volunteer infantry units organized in response to

President William McKinley's initial request for volunteer units during the Spanish-American War.

While not used in combat, the regiment was destined to play a brief role in the occupation of Cuba shortly after Spain's formal surrender overseeing the transfer of Spanish troops out of two Cuban provinces, providing regional security and supporting humanitarian activities.

The call up of state volunteers saw Kentucky State guard units converge in early May on Lexington. A camp was established outside of town at the Woodland Park where the units were discharged from state service and enrolled into Federal service. The First, Second and Third Kentucky filled the state's quota in response to President McKinley's call. A fourth regiment was organized later.

Colonel Thomas J. Smith was named to command the Third Kentucky. His medical staff consisted of Major Frank Boyd, Captain Austin Bell and Captain Nevill M. Garrett. The latter were mustered into U.S. service on May 10.

Among those stepping forward to serve was Logan Feland of Owensboro. Working as an architect in New York, he returned to Kentucky to command his hometown company. According to one source, Feland "was the last man in the world you would ever have picked out to be a soldier – a tall, skinny, slouchy Kentuckian, who couldn't be serious three minutes at a time". He arrived home on April 25th, screened his volunteers and selected 84 men to form the company which eventually became Company F, Third Kentucky Volunteer Infantry Regiment.[1]

---

[1] **Kentucky Marine: Major General Logan Feland and the Making of the Modern USMC** by David J. Bettez. (Lexington: University of Kentucky Press) 2014. See Chapter 2, 'Spanish War Service'. Feland's company was designated Company H in state service and redesignated 'F' in Federal service.

The Owensboro, Madisonville and Henderson volunteer companies left by train for Lexington on May 7. The Third Kentucky encamped at Camp Collier in Lexington where they were barracked in the Tattersall Racetrack barns.[2]

The units organized and drilled at Lexington. Their day started at 6 a.m. and ended at 10 p.m. with a full schedule in between.[3]

Daily Training Schedule

Morning

6:00 am	Reveille and Roll Call
6:15 am	Sick Call
6:15 am	Exercises
6:45 am	Recall
7:00 am	Breakfast
8:00 am	First Sergeant's call
8:30 am	Guard Mount; Fatigue duty was initiated immediately after the guard mount was posted.
9:30 am	Company Drill
11:30 am	Recall
11:30 am	Non-commissioned officer's school.

Afternoon

12:00 noon	Dinner
3:00 pm	Company Drill
4:00 pm	Recall
5:00 pm	Battalion Drill
6:00 pm	Recall
6:30 pm	Supper
9:30 pm	Tattoo
9:45 pm	Call to Quarters
10:00 pm	Taps

---

[2] Ibid; The initial authorization was for 84 men per company. This was later increased to 106.

[3] *The (Paris, Ky) Bourbon News*, May 13, 1898, 'News from Camp Collier', page 4.

The new state troops also learned the new language of the regular army. Each war brings its own terms, some of which are natural carry-overs from previous wars or experience. The men Camp Collier learned a whole new vocabulary.[4]

Slang Term	**Meaning**
Rookies	Enlisted men (probably 'new' men)
Dough Boys	Infantry Companies
Strong Boys	Artillery
Long Tom	Springfield Rifle
Sky Pilot	Chaplain
The Mill	Guardhouse
Sheepskin	Fiddler Drummer
Wind Jammer	Trumpeter
No. 4	A right hand salute without arms
Corner Bunks	Men who are hard to please. Corner bunks were reportedly the choicest position in an army post barracks

They even put words to the bugler's mess call:

> "Soupy, soupy, soup, soup
> Soup without a single bean
> Porky, porky, pork, pork
> With a streak of lean.
> Beefy, beefy, beef, beef.
> Seldom to be seen"

The men lived on a diet of salt pork for the first week until the acting Commissary of Subsistence could place an order for fresh beef. Over 2,000 loaves of bread were also being provided by local merchants causing a 'bread famine' in Lexington's civilian community.

'Blanket tossing' was reported as active 'sport' causing two

---

[4] **Ibid. It is in the form of a letter dated May 12, 1898, page 4.**

injuries. This caused a senior officer to stop the practice to aovid injuries that might prevent men from performing military service. Captain Brinton B. Davis, Company I, Third Kentucky also had an accident, falling from his top bunk straining "his back severely" causing fears he might not pass the physical required to muster into Federal service.[5]

It was also during this period the companies of the Second and Third Kentucky regiments were re-lettered. The companies were mustered into Federal service based on the seniority of their company Captains with the oldest companies mustering in first. For the Third Kentucky, the new system was publicly reported as follows:

New Federal Company	**Old State Company**	Community
A Captain James A. Burchfield[6]	E	Madisonville
B Captain Samuel Clark	A	Bowling Green
C Captain David Y. Beckham	C	Bardstown
D Captain John Feland[7]	D	Hopkinsville
E Captain Logan Feland[8]	H	Owensboro

---

[5] *The Daily Kentuckian*, May 15, 1898, 'Boys In Blue'.
[6] **Sometimes reported as "Birchfield" and reported in the news report as "Buchfield". The name was corrected by the official records.**
[7] **Later resigned from the position and replaced by Captain Noel Gaines in command of Company E.**

New Federal Company	Old State Company	Community
F Captain Fleming G. Railey[9]	F	Glasgow
G Captain John G. Keown[10]	G	Hartford
H Captain Hugh L. Atkinson	K	Henderson
I Captain Brinton B. Davis[11]	I	Paducah
K Captain Allen W. Brewer[12]	L	Vanceburg
L Captain Frank W. B. Reynolds	M	Lexington
M Captain Nathaniel T. Howard[13]	B	Morgantown

This public organization did not hold up as men objected to the appointment of new officers whom they did not elect or approve. It was reported on May 19:

> *"the Third Regiment Kentucky Volunteers is on the verge of*

---

[8] **Reassigned to Command Company F. Logan Feland later became a Marine Corps Major General.**
[9] **Listed in official records as Captain of Federal Company G.**
[10] **Listed in official records as Captain of Federal Company D.**
[11] **Listed in official records as Captain of Federal Company K.**
[12] **Listed in official records as Captain of Federal Company M.**
[13] **Listed in official records as Captain of Federal Company I.**

revolution tonight. Politics is the cause of the demoralization. The Hopkinsville company has been disbanded and the Hartford company threatens the same, and the Henderson company will do likewise unless they are allowed to elect a successor to Lieutenant South, thrown out because of a hernia.

"The trouble in the Hopkinsville company dates from the resignation on Tuesday of Captain John Feland, whose personal affairs forced such action. At the time E.B. Bassett was First Lieutenant and R.C. Payne was Second Lieutenant. The company held election Tuesday evening, and Gordon Nelson was elected as Captain with R.C. Payne as First Lieutenant, and Charles Prowse as Second Lieutenant. These names were sent to Governor Bradley for approval and commission. This the Governor refused, and appointed Noel Gaines, of Frankfort, to be Captain and Dr. H.L. Casey, of Lexington, to be First Lieutenant, placing Payne as Second Lieutenant.

"When they learned this today the members of the company almost to a man declared that they would not follow Gaines. The reasons stated are that he was once tried by Court-Martial for using the money paid to the Frankfort company for services at the Jackson and Walling hanging; that he was indicted in the Godfrey Hunter bribery affair at Frankfort during the hot senatorial contest, and the he lost his Captaincy of the Frankfort Company. They have no objections to Dr. Casey other than that they would prefer to follow men from their own town.

"After making these declarations about two-thirds of the company left camp, and, notwithstanding the facts that they had passed splendid physical examinations, boarded the train and went home.

"Mr. Bassett is in Hopkinsville tonight with about 30 recruits, for which he was arranging transportation, when he was wired of the disbandment. Whether he will bring them on is not known here.

> "*Another wrangle in the Third Regiment has arisen over the displacement of James R. Rash, of Henderson, as Battalion Adjutant and the appoint in his stead of A.G. Sharpley, a guard at the Frankfort Penitentiary, who a few months ago attained considerable notoriety on account of an affair with one of the female inmates, and for which he lost his place in the Second Regiment under Colonel Gaither.*
>
> *"The officers of the Third favor Rash, and a petition to the Governor in his behalf is being circulated in the regiment.*
>
> *"There has been also much desertion in the Third because of the appointment of Eastern Kentucky men as officers in many of the companies.*
>
> *"Aside from the Madisonville company there is scarcely one that has its minimum quota of 77, and men are being recruited to keep up the company to muster."*[14]

Captain John Feland's resignation from Hopkinsville's Company D, the Latham Light Guards, was motivated because he was allegedly drunk on duty. The Kentucky Adjutant General D.R Collier noted the inebriated Captain allowed his company to become disorganized and "substantially disbanded".

Through pressure from Feland's father and brother Logan, the Adjutant General directed John Feland proceed to Hopkinsville "without delay" with members who did not wish to enlist and allowed him to reorganize his company so it could be employed in state service. The Adjutant General also authorized Capt. Gaines and Lieutenant Casey to raise a company to take the place of Feland's company using the 30

---

[14] *The Daily Kentuckian*, May 21, 1898, 'Further Details of Co. D Muddle' and 'Reports Conflicting'.

men remaining of Feland's old company as the core cadre. This dwindled to 20 men.[15] Feland later publicly apologized for his personal failures, resigned his commission and tried to redeem his behavior by enlisting in the First Illinois Cavalry where he eventually became the First Sergeant of Company H in that unit.[16]

Noel Gaines bears special mention. At 29 years of age, he had already served in the militia for 13 years. He had commanded a detachment of the Kentucky National Guard and in that capacity helped break up "lawless gangs led by the famous Will Howard, the Turners, Eversoles and Frenches, putting an end to family feuds which had made the State notorious, and restoring public ordered in the 'moonshine' districts." As a person he was described as "modest, courteous and obliging". Gaines was from a different section of the state as the company he was to command and this caused friction. In addition to the other allegations, which appear politically motivated, Gaines was derisively described as one of Governor Bradley's "understrappers" thus leading to his gubernatorial appointment to command a company. A May 20 meeting of Hopkinsville's leading citizens was called to pass a resolution to put political pressure on the Governor to reverse his appointment. In that meeting Gaines was reportedly cited as "unfit to command a company of gentlemen or even to be their associates." The resolution called for the return of the company if they could not elect their own officers.[17]

---

[15] *The Daily Kentuckian*, May 21, 1898, 'As To Capt. Feland'; *The Daily Kentuckian*, May 22, 1898, 'Captain Feland Back'.
[16] *The (Earlington, Ky) Bee*, May 26, 1898, 'Company D's Trouble', page 3; *The Daily Kentuckian*, July 2, 1898, 'Sergeant Feland: Company D's Late Captain Enlists in An Ohio Company', page 4; *The Daily Kentuckian*, May 20, 1898, 'Company D Goes To Pieces'.
[17] Ibid, *Daily Kentuckian*, May 21; *The Frankfort (Ky) Roundabout*, April 15, 1899. Much of the background information originated with an article in the March 27, 1899 *Havana (Cuba) Daily Advertiser*.

Governor Bradly responded he had not commissioned anyone to command the company "as there is no one there to command" and stated Captain Feland was on his way home with troops who did not want to enlist into Federal service and the citizens committee "should address your complaint to Capt. Feland and those who desire to go home rather than to me."[18]

Press reports and letters to the editor indicate that the inability of Company D to elect their own Captain, as was practice in the State Guard, was an affront to the liberty of the men and was the main reason they walked away. In time the new Company D was filled by men from Carlisle, Frankfort and Hopkinsville. It was, as the local paper pointed out, not a 'Hopkinsville Company'. Likewise, the majority of the old Company D – the Latham Light Guards -- returned to Hopkinsville, reorganized and offered their services to the state only to be told by Governor Bradley that it was too late[19]

On May 24 the Third Kentucky Regiment's re-organization was listed, as follows:

New Federal Company	Old State Company	Community
E Captain James A. Burchfield	A	Madisonville
A Captain Samuel Clark	B	Bowling Green
C Captain David Y. Beckham	C	Bardstown

---

[18] Ibid, *Daily Kentuckian*, May 21.
[19] *The (Hopkinsville) Daily Kentuckian*, May 26, 1898, page 4; *The Daily Kentuckian*, May 24, 1898, 'Military Matters" Original Company D Anxious to Enlist', page 1.

New Federal Company	Old State Company	Community
G Captain John G. Keown	D	Hartford
D Captain Noel Gaines	E	Hopkinsville
H Captain Logan Feland	F	Owensboro
F Captain Fleming G. Railey	G	Glasgow
I Captain Hugh L. Atkinson	H	Henderson
B Captain Nathaniel T. Howard	I	Morgantown
K Captain Brinton B. Davis	K	Paducah
M Captain Frank W. B. Reynolds	L	Lexington
L Captain Allen W. Brewer	M	Vanceburg

Captain Gaines proved to be a highly efficient and capable officer. In July 1898 while the unit was in Chickamauga he was appointed to the staff of General Frederick Dent Grant, son of former President U.S. Grant, to serve as Provost Marshal. When the unit moved to Lexington he was appointed to General Sanger's staff serving the same function for the First Army Corps. His work in keeping order in the camps and surrounding area impressed the citizens of Lexington. They presented him "with a fine gold mounted sword" in token of their appreciation.

When General Joseph Cabell Breckinridge, Sr.[20] became Inspector General of the Army, he placed Gaines on his staff, also as Provost Marshal. When General James H. Wilson[21] took command of the First Army Corps, he obtained Gaines' services, also as Provost Marshal. When the Army moved to Columbus and was placed under General William Ludlow's command, he kept Gaines as Provost Marshal.[22] The people of that city were likewise impressed by Gaines' work and would present him a medal as "a token of the gratitude and esteem".[23]

The regiment apparently was briefly considered for movement to Washington, DC to support coastal defense but no actions were taken. Shortly after that and following a period of reorganization, the Third Kentucky's Colonel Thomas J. Smith announced his revised regimental staff.[24]

---

[20] Breckinridge, 56 years old, was a Union officer in the Civil War and the first cousin to Confederate Vice-President John C. Breckinridge.

[21] Wilson was about 61 years of age and had been a Union Major General in the Civil War.

[22] Ludlow, age 54, was a Union Army veteran and engineer breveted to the rank of Lieutenant Colonel in the Civil War. He served in the plains Indian Wars and would eventually command in the Philippines before dying in 1901 of tuberculosis contracted while serving in Cuba in 1898.

[23] *The Daily Kentuckian*, May 21, 1898, 'Further Details of Co. D Muddle'; *The Frankfort (Ky) Roundabout*, April 15, 1899. Much of the background information originated with an article in the March 27, 1899 *Havana* (Cuba) *Daily Advertiser*.

[24] *The (Earlington, Ky) Bee*, May 26, 1898, 'Third Regiment', page 3; see also *The Daily Kentuckian*, May 25, 1898, 'Mustering the Third', page 1.

Colonel, Commanding	Thomas J. Smith[25]
Lieutenant Colonel	Jouett Henry[26]
Surgeon/Major	Frank Boyd
First Assistant Surgeon	Austin Bell
Second Assistant Surgeon	Neville M. Garrett
Chaplain/Captain	Frank M. Thomas
Adjutant/First Lieutenant	Robert S. Mitchell[27]
Quartermaster/1st Lt	Frank L. Strange

---

[25] Thomas Jefferson Smith (born May 21, 1843 in Warren County, Ky., died March 21, 1904, Bowling Green, Warren County, Ky) Wife- Ella Bowden Wright Smith (1848-1916). Buried Fairview Cemetery, Bowling Green, Warren County, Kentucky. See the *Paducah Sun*, March 21, 1904, 'Col. Smith Dead: Well Known Commander of the Third Regiment No More' "Bowling Green, Ky., March 21 – Colonel T.J. Smith, Commander for many years of the Third Kentucky Regiment, state militia, and one of the best known men in the state, died this morning at his home here from Bright's disease, after a long illness. He was a banker and a prominent man, also a member of the Elks and Masons."; Find A Grave Memorial #74549533 as Thomas Jefferson Smith. He was a businessman and prominent citizen in Bowling Green, Kentucky where he served as Mayor from 1888-1891. See City of Bowling Green website: https://archive.bgky.org/20140501/www.bgky.org/citycommission/mayor_history_five.html

[26] Jouett Henry was born August 26, 1861 in Hopkinsville, Christian County, Kentucky and died February 25, 1942 in the same community. He served as Adjutant General of Kentucky from 1923-1924 under Governor William J. Fields. He is buried in Riverside Cemetery in Hopkinsville, Old Section, Lot 130. Find a Grave Memorial 30594126.

[27] Robert Stockton Mitchell was born September 7, 1870 in Bowling Green, Warren County, Kentucky and died January 11, 1942 in St. Louis City, Missouri. In 1912 he was named the Chief Special Agent form the Missouri Pacific Railroad. He later served as head of the U.S. railroad administration special agents in World War I. He was the organizer and served two times as the chairman of the special service department of the American Railway Association. He is buried in Fairview Cemetery in Bowling Green. See Find A Grave Memorial 26580368.

Battalion Majors	Edward H. Watt
	George C. Saffarans
	David C. Colson
First Lieutenants/ Battalion Adjutants	Getty E. Snell
	Joseph S. Simcox
	Arthur G. Sharpley
Sergeant-Major	M.F. Martin

Three deserters, two from Company E, were drummed out of camp about this time. It was reported, "These deserters are denounced as cowards and scoundrels, particularly as they lived off the company two weeks at home, got transportation to Lexington and lived off the Government two weeks longer then deserted at the last moment...the officers are 'glad to get rid of such cowards and mischief makers'."[28]

On May 25 the units began the redeployment to Camp Thomas on the Chickamauga battlefield in northern Georgia which was then serving as a concentration and training location for volunteer U.S. Army units preparing to deploy to the war. The Third Kentucky departed Lexington for Camp Thomas on June 1 arriving on June 2.

---

[28] Ibid, *Bee*, May 26, 1898.

CHAPTER 2

CAMP THOMAS

Camp Thomas faced rapid growth and was soon hosting over 60,000 troops. The lack of organization led to unsanitary conditions and contaminations of water supplies. Typhoid fever became rampant. Troops were sick and solutions were needed. Further, soldiers were not getting paid or receiving adequate food supplies. These conditions set the stage for disruptions in good order and discipline. These conditions also led to a series of Congressional inquiries.

Congress later directed the U.S. Surgeon General, who directed Major Walter Reed, Major Victor C. Vaughan and Major Edward O. Shakespeare, to conduct an investigation on the origin and spread of typhoid fever in U.S. military camps during the war.[29] Their report provides details on Camp Thomas' medical challenges.

The Third Kentucky had 63 medical cases in June. Dr. Bell

---

[29] <u>Report on the Origins and Spread of Typhoid Fever in U.S. Military Camps during the Spanish War of 1898</u> (Washington: Government Printing Office) 1904. Document No. 757, 58th Congress, Second Session.

reported the main diseases were diarrhea, mumps and measles. He wrote,

> *"Improper cooking and the purchasing of improper articles from hucksters caused the first. A daily rigid inspection of the kitchens, with proper attention to cooking and prohibiting the sale of undesirable articles soon checked the diarrhea. We had our contagious cases isolated from the rest of the command, placed guards around them, and kept them there until the infective period had passed."*[30]

The July report reveals the Third Kentucky has had "a few cases of typhoid fever". These were not treated in the Third's camp but sent to the larger Army hospital. Dr. Bell said the German measles and mumps have "afflicted the command" and "malarial fevers are quite prevalent." He had a total of 87 medical cases in July, 44 of those remained from June admissions. Two persons died, ten were transferred to other hospitals and ten people were discharged while 47 were returned to duty during the month.

The Surgeon General report noted the Third Kentucky's sick cases on June 6 and June 12 were reported as intermittent malaria and were later assessed to be typhoid fever. Based on these two instances they concluded the Third Kentucky arrived in Chickamauga with typhoid fever already in its ranks. They further assessed that up to July 28, the Third Kentucky had 39 probable cases of typhoid fever yet only six were diagnosed as such and one death was reported from the disease though they believe at least two men died of the disease.

Dr. Bell later disagreed with these findings stating "I do not think he regiment was infected on leaving Lexington, for up

---

[30] **Third Kentucky Regiment, June 1898 Medical Report, quoted in <u>Typhoid Fever Report</u>, page 39.**

to June 28 not a single case presented itself with a suspicious fever."[31]

Colonel Smith took matters in his own hands and ordered a new camp laid out for the Third Kentucky to improve sanitation and organization. He later testified before the Congressional Commission appointed by the President to investigate the conduct of the War Department in the war with Spain.[32] In that appearance he said the regiment began getting uniforms at Camp Thomas about fifteen days after arrival and that arms – specifically Springfield rifles -- were not received until July 15, almost six weeks after arrival. He said the Third Kentucky had about 150 state issued rifles but the regiment was not fully equipped until around July 17th or ten days before departing for Newport News which was the intermediate stop before the planned Puerto Rico campaign.

Colonel Smith also addressed the water situation noting the water from Crawfish Spring was hauled to camp in barrels and some local wells were used. A pipeline was later run through the camp allowing water for cooking and bathing.

Third Kentucky Quartermaster Lieutenant Frank L. Strange also shed light on the Camp Thomas bivouac. He testified the regular Army quartermaster initially did not have uniforms at Camp Thomas to issue. When clothing arrived, it was issued to units piecemeal then prioritized for units slated to go to Cuba. Lieutenant Strange said, "They just got it in a little at a time, and sometimes you could only draw 15 or 20 blouses at a time." He noted that he had requested underclothes and

---

[31] Third Kentucky Regiment, June 1898 Medical Report, quoted in **Typhoid Fever Report**, page 42.

[32] **Report of the Commission Appointed By the President To Investigate the Conduct of the War Department in the War with Spain**, 8 Volumes, (Washington: Government Printing Officer) 1900. Colonel Smith's testimony is in Volume 4, Testimony of Colonel Thomas J. Smith, page 1024-1027.

new tents for the command but after a month they were still waiting for delivery. He also said the unit had to acquire tools from commercial vendors in the area because the Army could not supply them.[33]

Private William K. Twohig recalled the ration situation. He said,

> *"After we got to Chickamauga, the rations were very scarce until June of July. The boys all got together and we went to see Colonel Smith about their eatables – I do not think I was present – I didn't go with them at all – and the next day the rations improved wonderfully…The lieutenant-colonel told the boys to go back and he would see what was the matter. We fared very well. We had rice, tomatoes, and potatoes, that we had never seen before, and fresh beef."*[34]

Thomas Taylor Thomas, a native of North Carolina, was in Company A of the Third Kentucky and was one of many who became sick while at Chickamauga. He enlisted without telling his parents and finally wrote them on July 11, 1898 from Chickamauga:

> *"Dear Mother and Father – It has been a good while since I wrote to you. The reason was that I have been moving about so much for the last two months or more. I am well at present, but I have just gotten over a hard spell of pneumonia. I was in the Hospital at Lexington, Ky. five weeks and came to Chickamauga before I was able to get about much. I belong to the 3<u>rd</u> <u>Ky.</u> <u>Volunteers</u> – <u>Co. A</u>. I don't want you to be uneasy about me for I don't think I am liable to get into much danger. The War will not last much longer I don't think for what Sampson and Shafter is doing for the Spaniards over in Cuba is*

---

[33] Ibid, Testimony of Lt. Frank L. Strange, p1065-1067.
[34] **Testimony of Private William K. Twohig, November 1, 1898, Investigation of the Conduct of the War with Spain. Volume 4, pages 1087-1088.**

a plenty.[35]

"*I am also afraid I will not get to go to Cuba at-all. I want to go to Cuba to see the country and I want Uncle Sam to pay my way. But I can't say that I want to face any Spanish bullets. And if I do get into a battle I shall surely try to take to the safest place. I will never act foolhardy you may rely upon that.*

"*When I left Joe's, I told him if he got a letter from you to ans. [answer] it and let me know how you all were getting along. And I recd [received] a letter from him some days ago and he said he has gotten one from you and had answered it. He said he told you I was off somewhere. He would not tell you I was in the army and I thought I would write you today and let you know where I was. I joined May 7 at Madisonville and all of the Ky. troops mustered in the U.S. Service at Lexington and we all was kept there for six weeks. And I in the meantime taken the pneumonia. I had a very hard spell. I was unconscious for a week during the time. I had the very best of attention and a doctor to see me 3 times per day. Preston Taylor is in the 1st Arkansas Regt and is camped in 4 hundred yards of where we are camped.*

"*We are camped on the very ground the great battle was fought in 1863. When so many was killed I guess you read about it during the war. You can find bullets and teeth all around here now. And old trees are full of bullets.*

"*The Government has bought all of Chickamauga battle ground and Missionary Ridge and converted it into a park. They have cannons mounted on Iron Wheels that shows where every battery was located.*
"*They have monuments for miles around erected in honor of the*

---

[35] Rear Admiral William T. Sampson was early on in the forefront of the fight. He directed the blockade of Cuba and the landing of General William Rufus Shafter's V Army Corps at Daiquiri. Sampson was in command of the U.S. Navy at the battle of Santiago Bay on July 3, 1898, the largest naval engagement in the war.

Killed, both Federal, and Confederate.

"Well I must close. Write as soon as you get this.
"Give my love & respects to all, love your son;

Thos Taylor
Co. A 3rd Ky. Vol.[36]

Alerted for Cuba

On July 3rd General Rufus Shafter demanded the surrender of Spanish forces in Santiago. He had earlier asked the War Department for 20,000 reinforcements to replace the many men who already been prostrated by disease. While the news for reinforcements was received in Chickamauga the last week of June, the official order arrived on the afternoon of July 3rd. Among those identified for service were the First Division of the First Army Corps. The Third Kentucky was in the Third Brigade of the First Division.

According to news reports for July 3rd,

> *"The regiments of the First division were inspected this evening and are ready to move. The others have been kept busy since the order to prepare for the field came a week ago, getting rid of their excess of equipment and clothing, and it will require very little time to break camp and depart. In anticipation of this order the railroads have been accumulating cars at this point for a week. The Western & Atlantic railroad is crowded with Pullman cars. It is stated tonight that there are thirty trains of twenty cars each on the tracks here ready to transport troops. The regiments will embark at Rossville and Ringgold, to ensure speedy transportation, as was done when the regulars were moved south, and it thought by the railroad authorities that they can move the*

---

[36] ***William Thomas Taylor Papers*, Letter dated July 11, 1898.**

20,000 men in two days."[37]

Target practice was ordered for the affected troops to increase proficiency in marksmanship. The movement, while anticipated in the press, was delayed. On July 13th, General Shafter discussed the surrender of Spanish troops with the Santiago commander who capitulated on July 17th. The troops in Chickamauga would not be needed for active operations in Cuba.

To Puerto Rico

On July 18, Spain asked for a ceasefire using France as the intermediary with the United States. This began the discussions to establish negotiations for a peace protocol. The news did not stop U.S. military operations however. On July 20 the War Department announced the dispatch of 30,000 soldiers for the "Porto Rican army of invasion" under General Nelson Miles. The Third Kentucky, as part of the First Army Corps, was among those listed for active operations.[38]

---

[37] *The Seattle Post-Intelligencer*, July 4, 1898, 'Troops Detailed to Reinforce Shafter', page 3; *Topeka State Journal*, July 4, 1898, 'Advance from Camp Thomas'. "Although the officials at headquarters continue to maintain great secrecy in regard to the movement of troops from here to Cuba. It is generally believed that the movement will begin tomorrow. Fifteen regiments are under emergency orders and the indications are that the start will be made at once. Preparations are being rushed today and a rare scene of activity is witnessed. The regiments which go out first are as follows:…Third Kentucky…", page 8; *The Wichita Daily Eagle*, July 5, 1898, 'Shafter Reinforcements', page 2; *Kansas City Journal*, July 4, 1898, 'The Third To Go: Kansas City Volunteers Ordered to Santiago', page 8

[38] *The Copper Country (Illinois) Evening News*, July 20, 1898, '30,000 Soldier: Will Take Part in the Porto Rican Invasion', page 4; *The (NY) Sun*, July 27, 1898, 'Troops From Camp Thomas', page 4; *The (Washington) Times*, July 29, 1898, 'Leaders of the Army', page 3; *The (NY) Sun*, July 28, 1898, 'Troops for the Front: More Soldiers Sent East from Chickamauga Park', page 2.

Brigadier General Frederick Dent Grant, son former General and President U.S. Grant, was assigned to command the Third Brigade of General James H. Wilson's First Army Corps on July 23rd. The Third Brigade consisted of the First and Third Kentucky Infantry and the Fifth Illinois. One report noted,

> *"Two of the regiments in Gen. Grant's brigade were recruited in Kentucky and it may be justly regarded as one of the notable incidents of this precedent-making war that the son of U.S. Grant should lead to battle the first Southern troops sent into active service."*

It further noted the designated Kentucky commanders, Colonel John B. Castleman of the First Kentucky and Colonel Edgar H. Gaither of the Second Kentucky, filling in for the sick Colonel Smith of the Third, "fought under Confederate colors." [39]

---

[39] *Barre (Vermont) Evening Telegram*, July 23, 1898, 'General Grant Given Command', page 2 ; *The (Washington) Times*, July 29, 1898, 'Leaders of the Army', page 3; Colonel Castleman was a Major in the Confederate Army and helped form the Second Kentucky Cavalry under John Hunt Morgan. He was captured in October 1864 and sentenced to be executed for spying but Lincoln stayed the execution. By 1883 he was the Adjutant General of Kentucky, commanded the First Kentucky Volunteers in the Spanish—American War, participated in the invasion of Puerto Rico and was promoted to a brigadier general of U.S. Volunteers serving as military governor of that island. He died in 1918. He wrote an autobiography entitled <u>Active Service</u> (Louisville, Ky: Courier-Journal Job Printing Company, Publishers) 1917; Edgar Hutchinson Gaither was born November 7, 1852 and died in 1938. As he would have been ten years old in 1862, he would have been one of the Confederacy's 'boy soldiers'. His Confederate service cannot positively be ascertained with a compiled service records search. As a side note, Isaac Stamps Alexander (November 20, 1855-October 11, 1919) of Company I, 2nd Kentucky Volunteer Infantry was the grand-nephew of former Confederate President Jefferson Davis. Alexander was chosen to carry Regimental Stars and Stripes and

Grant drilled his troops on July 25th. According to one news report, the brigade

> *"went on an extended order drill Saturday from 6 o'clock a.m. until nearly noon. General Grant mounted a cannon and directed the movement of the troops from that elevation. The movements of the troops consisted of manoeuvers similar to those employed in time of battle."*[40]

Orders were received on July 25th for movement of the first two brigades of the First Corps, but nothing on the Third Brigade containing the Third Kentucky. It was reported the Kentucky regiments were "short on ordnance supplies".[41]

Grant's brigade and the Third Kentucky began movements on July 27 to Newport News, Virginia to support American operations in Puerto Rico. The Third Kentucky was the last regiment of the brigade to leave. They were sent to Camp Grant along the James River.[42] The movement of the Fifth Illinois was also cancelled by the Secretary of War, possibly because they were not 'combat ready', and the 160th Indiana was sent to Newport News in their stead, changing the

---

was deluged with autograph seekers after his appointment was announced. He was later killed when struck by an automobile. See *The (Paris, Ky) Bourbon News*, May 13, 1898, 'News from Camp Collier', page 4 and *The (Paris, Ky) Bourbon News*, May 20, 1898, 'News from Camp Collier', page 4.

[40] *The True (Paw Paw, Michigan) Northerner*, July 27, 1898, 'Gen. Grant Drills His Troops', page 2.

[41] *The (NY) Sun*, July 26, 1898, 'Orders for First Corps', page 3.

[42] It was reported on July 30 that Grant's Brigade had arrived and would likely embark on the transports Alamo, Hudson, and Rio Grande. That did not happen. See *Barre (Vermont) Evening Telegram*, July 30, 1898, 'The St. Paul Sails', page 2; *The Salt Lake Herald*, July 27, 1898, 'Grant's Brigade: Sone of His Father Anxious to Make a Record', page 2.

brigade makeup.⁴³

Unfortunately rampant illness had taken its toll on the Third Kentucky. It was reported on August 2nd that eighty men in the brigade were sick in Newport News with thirty of them in the Third Kentucky. At least two died including John F. Sproule, Company I, who succumbed to injuries resulting from a brain concussion. Also dead was First Sergeant Frank Brewer, Company M, who succumbed to typhoid fever caught at Chickamauga. Brewer was the son of the Company Captain. Many of the men were so sick they were sent to the hospital at Fort Monroe.⁴⁴

Dr. Bell reported,

> *"While in Virginia our regiment remained in shelter tents for sixteen days without any shade to protect the men from the scorching sun. Much sickness developed, and in most instances the onset was sudden, and an initial chill was very common, followed by a temperature of 104 to 105 [degrees] F. Often on first seeing the patient an excessively high temperature would be found, with the history of feeling perfectly well until that day. Many of these cases of sudden incipiency subsequently proved to be typhoid. Only those cases were diagnosed malaria or typhoid which were undoubtedly these diseases. The undetermined class consisted mostly of suspected typhoid cases.⁴⁵*

---

⁴³ *The Kansas City Journal*, July 28, 1898, 'A Grievous Disappointment: Illinois Troops Have Orders to Go to Porto Rico Countermanded for Second Time', page 3; *The Salt Lake Herald*, July 28, 1898, 'A Mutiny At Chickamauga', page 2. The Third Kentucky entrained from the Rossville depot near Chickamauga. The report also noted the 5th Illinois was reported by its Colonel as not ready for battle and this prevented their deployment. Later news reports clarified their commander made no such recommendation.
⁴⁴ *The Daily Kentuckian*, August 2, 1898, 'Eighty Men Sick: Thirty of Them in the Third Kentucky – Two Dead'.
⁴⁵ Typhoid Fever Report, page 42, 'Communications from the Surgeons of the Third Kentucky Volunteer Infantry'.

Dr. Bell reported the Third Kentucky suffered typhoid fever, mumps and measles during the month of August. He wrote,

> *"Our typhoid was supposedly contracted at Chickamauga Park, Ga., probably from a contaminated water supply. All the regiments in the park suffered from this disease to a greater or less extent. The common water supply for the regiments in our brigade was from Crawfish Springs. Each regiment was supplied with a single well."*

He said isolating mumps and measles cases reduced the number of new cases but nearly one-fourth of the command was sick with something. His report shows 1,079 men in the regiment and a total of 245 hospital admissions, only two of which were carry-overs from the previous month. One man died and 28 were returned to duty but 166 were transferred to other hospitals. The Surgeon General's postwar report says the Third Kentucky assessed 98 of these cases occurring in Newport News were, in actuality, typhoid fever.[46]

Private Twohig also recalled the food and sanitation situation at Newport News describing conditions that might very well have contributed to unit illnesses. He said,

> *"In Newport News we had some company funds, and once or twice bought meat and potatoes. Our fresh meat came up to camp about 11 o'clock, and most of the time it was tainted. It came at such a time that it was meant for the cook to cook and handle it at once, and it got tainted."*

He said that occurred about two-thirds of time they were in Newport News. He said, "I was helping very often in the kitchen, and when it came we would put it immediately to boil it so as to save it."

---

[46] Third Kentucky Regiment, June 1898 Medical Report, quoted in <u>Typhoid Fever Report</u>, page 39-41

Twohig said his Company C cook was very good noting

> *"a great many of the boys from other camps came there and got something, and they said it was cooked in better shape than theirs…There was one thing I did not like here; our sinks [latrines] were in the neighborhood of 75 to 125 feet from the kitchen, and very frequently the stench was so offensive as to turn us all from eating, and there came a heavy rain, and the maggots just crawled out of the sinks and crawled into the kitchen."*[47]

The Third Kentucky's degree of combat readiness was also questioned leading Kentucky Governor W.O. Bradley to telegraph General H.C. Corbin on August 8: "Please let Third Kentucky go to Porto Rico. You will place many Kentuckians under lasting obligations by doing this."[48]

On August 9th the Secretary of War stopped the movement of reinforcements to Puerto Rico after General Miles reported by morning cable that he had enough troops there to finish taking the island. News reports indicated a provisional U.S. corps of 18 regiments would not be needed. It was thought however the Third Kentucky and one other regiment would be allowed to sail to join the rest of their division which had already departed.[49] This proved not to be the case however.

The Third Kentucky was in the process of embarking on August 10th when orders terminated. They were literally on board the ship making ready to sail. The termination of this

---

[47] Ibid, Twohig testimony.
[48] **Correspondence Relating to The War With Spains and Conditions Growing Out of the Same Including the Insurrection in the Philippine Islands,** in two Volumes (Washington: Government Printing Officer) 1902.
[49] *The Salt Lake Herald*, **August 10, 1898, 'No More Troops" General Miles Sends Word That He Has Enough', page 2.**

deployment had a negative impact on morale.[50]

While in Virginia a woman identified as Mrs. Flora Gowell organized local citizens to extend support and aid sick members of the Third Kentucky as well as their families. At least one of the Kentucky soldiers was buried near her home and "for three and one half years" Mrs. Gowell visited the grave of that soldier weekly "keeping it in good condition." In 1902, her kindness was remembered with a Joint Resolution of the Kentucky Legislature.[51]

On August 12 the U.S. and Spain signed an armistice leading to negotiations that would result in the final document termed the Treaty of Paris in December. On August 15th the Third Kentucky and 160th Indiana were ordered back to the Lexington encampment.[52]

Private Monroe Forgy

Private Monroe Forgy of Butler County, Kentucky was one medical problem that was overlooked when the unit moved out for Newport News. Forgy was a member of Company B and was at Camp Thomas in Chickamauga for well over a month when he became sick. After a week he was sent to a larger hospital where he appears to have been forgotten by his regiment. No accommodations were made for his care when the regiment left for Newport News. Through some

---

[50] *The (Washington, DC) Times*, August 11, 1898, 'Disgusted Illinois Troops: They Will Not Sail to Porto Rico on the Obdam'

[51] Journal of the Regular Session of the Senate of the Commonwealth of Kentucky (Louisville, Ky: The George G. Fetter Printing Company) 1902. Senate Resolution No. 5, Wednesday, January 15, 1902, page 93 and page 487; Acts of the General Assembly of the Commonwealth of Kentucky Passed (Louisville, Ky: George G. Fetter Printing Company) 1901, page 408-09, Resolution No. 19; see also *Richmond Times Dispatch*, January 25, 1902, 'Mrs. Flora Gowell Thanked: Newport News Lady Who Cared for Sick Soldiers', page 5,..

[52] *The (NY) Sun*, August 16, 1898, 'Troops for Manila Held Up', page 4.

oversight, he was abandoned.

Forgy laid on a cot, apparently did not communicate, did not eat nor was he attended and his hair reportedly became white. Further he had nothing on him that would give his identity. His actions "became suspicious and his talk rambling, and finally he became offensive because of his painful babble and moaning." Officers in the First Pennsylvania were able to get some doctors to examine Forgy whom they declared "insane" and directed he be sent to St. Elizabeth's insane asylum in Washington, D.C. The Pennsylvania officers arranged transportation, obtained an old uniform (as he reportedly had no clothes) and sent a two-man detail with him to make sure he arrived safely at the hospital. The commissary would not issue any food to Forgy so the two soldiers and sympathetic passengers ended up buying him food on the trip.

Forgy reportedly said nothing during the transit, stared into space and occasionally moaned. His uniform was old and worn out, his shoes were worn out and his socks "were little better than nothing". He also had a rubber poncho "for which he exhibited great affection". One news report quotes a Washington citizen as saying "this was the most disgraceful thing he had ever witnessed" and questioned why the man was allowed to travel.

Forgy was admitted into St. Elizabeth's on August 18. He was reportedly one of over 20 soldiers from the volunteer army diagnosed as insane. The news report said,

> *"It is claimed by those who have examined the Forgy case that an investigation into the causes leading up to the insane condition of the other twenty-two volunteer patients would bring to light some horrible truths about the treatment of the soldiers in the various camps throughout the country."*[53]

---

[53] *The (Washington) Times,* September 19, 1898, 'Here Horror Lies Hidden: Monroe Forgy, Insane and Forgotten, in St. Elizabeth's', page 5; It is possible Forgy suffered from some other ailment that

CHAPTER 3

THE 'BATTLE' OF LEXINGTON

By August 15, Brigadier General Joseph P. Sanger, commanding the Third Division of the U.S. First Army Corps was back in Lexington looking for camp sites.[54] The Clark and Wells farms were selected for newly established Camps Hamilton and Miles, respectively. The troops still at Camp Thomas were destined for Camp Hamilton as were the

---

impacted his behaviors as he appears to have recovered. A 'Find-A-Grave' entry has Monroe Perry Forgy, Company B, 3rd Kentucky Infantry and shows him as born in Quality, Kentucky on July 26, 1875 and dying in February 1945 in Waurika, Jefferson County, Oklahoma. A period obituary quoted on the site indicates he was a Waurika pioneer arriving in 1919. It further states he "saw service in the Philippine Islands and Cuba" and "spent 13 months in a Cuban hospital". He had two wives, fathered six children and over 20 grandchildren and was a devout man who was active in the Methodist Church. His headstone application indicates he enlisted on June 24, 1898 and was discharged October 11, 1898 and received a Federal pension (No. 1116598).

[54] Sanger, age 58, was a Union veteran and artilleryman of the Civil War with two brevets for gallantry.

troops coming in from Newport News.⁵⁵

The Third Kentucky arrived in Lexington beginning on August 16th. They were first stationed at Camp Miles and transferred to Camp Hamilton on September 17th as other units were sent home to demobilize. Before leaving Newport News, on the night of August 14th, a Sergeant McCue of the regiment was reported fatally stabbed in a crap game.⁵⁶

Each regiment formed a camp of long rows of tents. Wooden floors were later added. These were supplemented by a hospital, a post office averaging 20 to 25 thousand letters per day, commissary buildings and a corral for regimental animals. There were three telegraph services and even four or five pay phones for the troops. The camp was serviced by a railroad spur line from the Lexington and Eastern Railroad with regular passenger service.

The first week of September the War Department issued a list of volunteer regiments to be mustered out of Federal service and a list of those to be retained. The Third Kentucky Infantry was among the latter.⁵⁷

With hostilities over and no immediate prospect of overseas service many of the regiments petitioned to be disbanded and sent home. Discipline broke down and military authority was challenged. While it also had its difficulties the Third Kentucky's military professionalism and willingness to

---

[55] *The (Washington, DC) Times*, August 11, 1898, 'Disgusted Illinois Troops: They Will Not Sail to Porto Rico on the Obdam'
[56] *The Paducah Daily Sun*, August 15, 1898, 'Again to Lexington', page 1. There is no 'Sergeant McCue' listed on the 3rd Kentucky rosters. The only Kentucky 'McCue' is Private Harry C. McCue of the 4th Kentucky Infantry's band. There was a Sergeant William J. McHugh in Company H, 3rd Kentucky.
[57] *Kansas City Journal*, September 4, 1898 'Fate of the Volunteers', page 6.

perform occupation duty in Cuba led to its selection for retention.

A September news report indicated the Third Kentucky had a "guard mount" of 42 men who acted "as a police for the camp and sees that everything is in order on the grounds." Several officers were on leave and "mementos of the late Spanish-American War such as 'Remember the Maine', 'to h—l with Spain' were used to decorate the tents." The men attempted to organize a regimental band and replaced tents. Winter overcoats and other required articles were expected "at any time". [58]

In mid-September elements of the Third Kentucky were selected for a public relations event and sent to Nicholasville, Kentucky to help the town and Jessamine County celebrate its 100th anniversary. A Mrs. M.B. Arnett of the town's Centennial committee made the request to Division headquarters and it was granted.[59]

By September the unit had regained its strength totaling 1,265 men. Hospital admissions, while high at 90 new cases, was lower than the previous month. There were also 48 carry over cases. Mumps and measles were the main culprits and "all typhoid cases were removed from camp as quickly as possible". Malaria was also reported. Of these 61 were returned to duty, 50 were transferred to other hospitals and 12 were sent elsewhere leaving 15 remaining on sick report by the end of the month. Thirty of these were later assessed as likely typhoid.

Dr. Bell reported new sanitation procedures noting

---

[58] *The Paducah Daily Sun,* **September 13, 1898, 'Third Kentucky Notes'**
[59] *The Paducah Daily Sun,* **September 12, 1898, 'Third Kentucky: Will Participate in a Celebration at Nicholasville'.**

> "*our privies were kept in the best possible sanitary condition. Copperas (10 pounds to 10 galls of water) was used in each sink [latrine] once a day; 3 pounds of powdered copperas was also used. One bottle of chloride of lime to a bucket of water was used to the sinks three times a day. The floors, seats and walls of sinks have been scoured and mopped once a day with a solution of bichloride of mercury – 1 to 200. All tent floors have been cleaned daily with the same solution.*"[60]

These actions paid dividends for the health of the men. Captain Bell reported in October,

> "*Hygienic details in regards to the care of the sick have been carried out. Camp has been kept thoroughly cleaned, and the health of the regiment is greatly improved.*" He said malaria was responsible for most of the 114 new sick cases and "*rheumatism has furnished more cases than in previous months.*"[61]

By the end of the month only 24 people remained on sick report. The Surgeon General still reassessed that eight of the sick cases were possibly typhoid.

The 'Battle' of Lexington

A major event occurred while the unit was in Lexington and nearly pitted the Kentuckians in open combat with the Twelfth New York Volunteer Infantry. On the evening of Sunday, October 9th – near midnight -- Private Alva[62] Kitchen of Company H was on Provost Guard duty in the town of Lexington. The troops at Camp Hamilton had recently been paid and had been going into town to carouse. Near

---

[60] **Third Kentucky Regiment, September 1898 Medical Report, quoted in Typhoid Fever Report, page 39.**

[61] **Third Kentucky Regiment, October 1898 Medical Report, quoted in Typhoid Fever Report, page 39-40.**

[62] **Also variously reported as 'Alvie' or 'Alvi'. He was a volunteer under Captain Howard from Butler County, Kentucky. See 'Find A Grave' Memorial #98825454.**

midnight, Kitchen responded to a reported fight in one of the business establishments. Kitchen explained, "I came down Corrall street from Megowan, and saw a crowd of soldiers standing on Dewees street. I asked to see their passes."

Private Henry Nygran of Company B, Twelfth New York Volunteer Infantry produced an old pass that had belonged to a Private Henry Hefferman of Company L. Rather than be caught with a fake pass, Nygran got scared and took off running.

Kitchen said,

> *"I called to him twice to halt, but he did not heed the command, and I fired in the air to frighten him. He continued to run, then I fired the second shot, which struck him. He ran some distance before falling and I did not think that I had killed him, as I fired low. The man came out of a house on Dewees street, and when he started to run one of his shoes came off. I fired because I thought I was in the right…I shot the man because I had orders to shoot at any man who would not halt when ordered."*

Unknown to Kitchen, the orders had been changed at that morning's guard mount. According to a statement by the Third Kentucky's Provost Marshal Noel Gaines[63],

> *"Sunday morning at guard mount I went before the guard and gave them orders which came to me from General [Joseph C.] Breckinridge [commanding First Army Corps] with reference to*

---

[63] **Gaines was assigned as Provost Marshal for Lexington on August 23, 1898 and was responsible for maintaining order of the soldiers stationed in the area. In this capacity he worked with the local police and supervised a military guardhouse. Among his orders,** *"All men of this command found in the city without written pass properly signed by the regimental commanders will be arrested and returned to camp under guard."* **See Lexington Museum of History website: http://lexhistory.org/wikilex/spanish-american-war**

a guard using a gun—when to use it and when not to do so. I told the men when necessary to control these men to use their clubs or club the guns but never to use a bayonet or place a ball cartridge in the magazine unless they expected to fire the next moment to protect their lives." [64]

For some unexplained reason Kitchen was not present at the morning guard mount and did not get the instructions. Following the shooting Kitchen was arrested by the local Sheriff and jailed. The deceased soldier was initially reported as Henry Hefferman as that was the name on the pass. This was later corrected in press accounts to Nygran.

Around 7:30 p.m. the night on October 10th about 300 members of the Twelfth New York and reportedly the First Territorial and Third Mississippi Volunteer Infantry regiments decided they were going to town to break into the jail and hang or shoot Private Kitchen. The mob rioted at the camp train station for about an hour and shots were fired before military authority could be restored sometime after 9 p.m.[65] According to news reports an estimated 300 to 400 soldiers were armed with knives, pistols and clubs and captured a Lexington & Eastern Train. They were reportedly "not friendly to the provost guard, and especially do not like

---

[64] Also referenced as 'Nigren'. Nygran was a native of Brooklyn, New York and his remains were transferred there by train on Tuesday night, October 11. He mustered into Company B, 12th New York on June 28,1898; see also *The (Los Angeles) Herald*, 'Troops at Lexington: Draw Their Pay and Many Get Drunk', October 11, 1898, page 4; see also *The (Earlington, Kentucky) Bee*, October 13, 1898, 'Killed by Provost: Member of New York Regiment Shot by Alvie Kitchen', page 3; *The (New York) Sun*, October 11, 1898, 'New York Soldier Shot: Edward Nygren of the Twelfth Regiment Killed by a Provost Guard', page 7

[65] *Marietta (Ohio) Daily Leader*, October 12, 1898, 'Soldiers Riot: They Sought to Lynch Provost Guard Alvin Kitchen at Lexington, Ky.', page 4; See also *The Bourbon (Paris, Kentucky) News*, October 14, 1898, 'Soldiers Engage In A Riot', page 4

the Kentuckians"[66]

Reports credit a railroad dispatcher named Stevens for providing early warning of the pending riot to military authorities. He could see the mob and learned of their intent and immediately wired the Lexington Depot where a dispatcher named Tompkins informed Captain Noel Gaines, the provost marshal. Gaines ordered the train held at the camp and telephoned Brigadier General John A. Wiley then commanding in the absence of General Sanger.[67] Wiley contacted Colonel Robert Woodward Leonard commanding the 12th New York who mobilized his officers and about 200 men.[68] They went straight to the depot to engage the rioters.

Colonel Leonard reportedly told the men to get off the train. By this time the engine had been decoupled and was run up the track away from the passenger cars. The men refused to leave. Colonel Leonard gave the command to this guards to "club their guns and drive the rascals out of the coaches." Colonel Leonard led his officers and men onto the train cars where a wild melee took place involving clubs and knives. At least 50 of the rioters "fell unconscious or ran bleeding from the train to renew the fight on the depot platform."

One news report gives details of some of the words exchanged between an officer – reportedly Captain Willard Ames Holbrook, adjutant general on General Wiley's staff -- and one of the rioters.[69] Holbrook reportedly ordered all

---

[66] Ibid; *Owingsville (Kentucky) Outlook*, October 20, 1898, page 4
[67] Wiley was a Pennsylvanian who had served as an enlisted man in the Union Army and participated in the battle of Antietam.
[68] Leonard served as a Major and was brevetted to Lieutenant Colonel while serving with the Sixty-second New York Volunteer infantry during the Civil War.
[69] Holbrook of Wisconsin was born in 1860, graduated from the U.S. Military Academy in 1881 and served in the 1st and 3rd U.S. Cavalry before being named Assistant Adjutant General of U.S. Volunteers

peaceful soldiers back to camp when he first arrived at the depot. A corporal reportedly yelled out: *"All who do are cowards."*

Holbrook asked him to what regiment he belonged and he answered "The Big Four" to which the officer replied,

> *"... that was no way to speak to an officer. The solder made some reply and [Holbrook] grabbed him by the arm. The soldier tore away, leaving his coat sleeve in the captain's hands and drawing a pistol shot at [Holbrook]. The bullet missed [the officer]. The corporal then climbed under a car. Lieutenant Langdon followed him and was shot at twice. The soldier escaped. Many of the Twelfth New York regiment had to be clubbed into submission."*[70]

General Wiley eventually arrived with reinforcements and got control of the situation. According to one report, "When the men were finally put back into the regiment of the 13th New York they made a break for the pike, but were repulsed by a heavy guard from the Third Kentucky, 160th Indiana and Eighth Massachusetts." The camp was quarantined under the

---

on 12 May 1898. He served at Chickamauga Park, Lexington and as was Adjutant General in Matanzas, Cuba from January 1, 1899 until April 11 when his volunteer commission was vacated. He commanded a battalion of the 38th Infantry in the Philippines in 1900 where he received a brevet as Lieutenant Colonel for gallantry. He retired in 1924 as Major General and Chief of Cavalry. He died in 1932 and is buried in Arlington. See Cullum's **Biographical Register of the Officers and Graduates of the United States Military Academy**, (1891) Vol. III, p388. http://digital-library.usma.edu/cdm/compoundobject/collection/p16919coll3/id/14017/rec/2

[70] *Jamestown (North Dakota) Weekly Alert*, October 13, 1898, 'Riotous Soldiers', page 8; *Rock Island (Illinois) Argus*, October 11, 1898, 'Mob Law In the Army', page 1; see also *Graham (Arizona) Guardian*, October 21, 1898, 'McCord's Regiment in Action'; *The (Washington) Evening Star*, October 11, 1898, 'Soldiers In A Riot', page 7.

guard of the Eighth Massachusetts Regiment but a part of the mob that escaped was making its way into town on foot. Because of this two companies of the Third Kentucky were moved into Lexington to assist the provost guard and help protect the jail. Between 40 to 50 soldiers were posted at the jail along with the jailer, the Sheriff and his deputies, all armed with Winchester rifles. The entire 160th Indiana Regiment was directed to patrol the city streets and reportedly went "through every restaurant, saloon and open house in town and are arresting every soldier." Officers were "arrested the same as privates…over 500 were arrested."[71] Another report stated "Kitchen is badly scared and fears he will yet be lynched." It further noted that "Captain Gaines, in charge of the provost guard…ordered his men to not shoot unless compelled to do so but when they did to take aim to kill."[72] It was believed at the time that Kitchen would get the death penalty.

There were other shootings and drunken brawls that night. In one instance a soldier identified as Private Bailey of Company A, Third Engineers Regiment, was also shot by the Provost Guard that night, seriously wounded in the thigh. According to news reports, he was attempting to escape the guard when shot. His "hip bone was shattered." The leg had to be amputated.[73]

On October 13 ten men from the Twelfth New York accosted Sergeant A. McClelland of Company C, Third Kentucky and seriously beat him, injuring his spine and

---

[71] Ibid; *The Brooklyn (New York) Daily Eagle*, October 11, 1898, 'New York Soldiers An Avenging Mob', page 8.
[72] *Rock Island (Illinois) Argus*, October 11, 1898, 'Mob Law In the Army', page 1;
[73] Ibid, *The Brooklyn (New York) Daily Eagle*; The Leadville, Colorado *Herald Democrat*, October 10, 1898, 'Saturnalis of Soldiers Crimes', page 1

requiring hospitalization.⁷⁴ Military authorities decided to delay Kitchen's trial because of this incident and fear for a larger outbreak of violence between the regiments.⁷⁵ Two Lexington police officers were also reportedly beaten.

That same day the civil Judge Frank A. Bullock indicated he was inclined to consider the alleged offense a military matter and that Kitchen should be tried by a military court. Judge Bullock was cited as thinking "it would be an injustice to place the expense of trying the case on the state." The report speculated the court would turn Kitchen over to the military ruling the court has no jurisdiction. The news report said,

> *"This is just what the 12ᵗʰ New York men do not want. They feel that the provost guard will be backed up by the commanding general and that Kitchen will be acquitted before a court-martial, whereas they hoped a jury would convict him of murder or at least manslaughter."*⁷⁶

The initial hearing was delayed because of the riots. When it finally reached court on October 18ᵗʰ the Lexington City Attorney recommended charges be dismissed because "Provost Marshal Gaines was present with a military warrant for the arrest of Kitchen. The court dismissed the charge and Kitchen was placed under military arrest" for an Army determined to hold a general court-martial.⁷⁷

---

⁷⁴ The Third Kentucky's regimental roster does not show a Sergeant McClelland. Company C did contain a QM Sergeant James M. McGill. A Sergeant William J. McHugh was in Company H.
⁷⁵ *The (New York) Sun*, October 14, 1898, 'Assaulted By Twelfth New York Men', page 4; The Salt Lake Herald, October 14, 1898, 'More Trouble at Lexington', page 2
⁷⁶ *Marietta (Ohio) Daily Leader*, 'Guard Kitchen's Trial', October 12, 1898, page1; see also *Wheeling (West Virginia) Daily Intelligencer*, October 13, 1898, 'Question of Jurisdiction', page 4.
⁷⁷ *Los Angeles Herald*, October 20, 1898, 'A Military Trial', page 3; *The (Washington, DC) Times*, October 19, 1898, 'Tried by Court

The 22-year-old Kitchen received good treatment while incarcerated. One report says he was "supplied with meals from a Lexington hotel by order of the Quartermaster of his regiment."[78]

The court martial was finally held on October 31, 1898 in Lexington. Eleven witnesses testified on Kitchen's behalf stating Kitchen was not present when the Provost Guard received orders that they were not to shoot except in self-defense. There was no public report of the General Officer's affirmation of the court martial findings but news reports suggest Kitchen was cleared of any wrongdoing in the performance of his duty.[79]

Newspaper Profile

During their time in Lexington, with the main fighting over, the Third Kentucky petitioned to muster out rather than mark time 'camping out'. Kentucky's governor made several appeals to the President and the Army to use the Kentucky troops. As a result, the troops were considered for Occupation Duty in Cuba. When the Second Kentucky disbanded, recruits from that regiment wishing to do additional service were mustered into the Third Kentucky to bring the regiment up to full strength.

The *Paducah Daily Sun* republished a *Lexington Leader* profile on the regiment in its November 1, 1898 edition giving a

---

Martial: Private Kitchen Dismissed and Rearrested Yesterday', page 1.
[78] *The (Earlington, Kentucky) Bee*, October 20, 1898, page 2, column one item, no headline.
[79] *Jamestown (North Dakota) Weekly Alert*, October 13, 1898, 'Riotous Soldiers', page 8; *The (New York) Sun*, 'Provost Guard Kitchen's Trial: Testimony Favors the Soldier Accused of Killing Private Nigran', November 1, 1898, page 7; The Lexington History Museum website says the shooting was ruled "in the line of duty". Alva Kitchen died in 1914 at the age of 38. He is buried in New Midway Church Cemetery in his native Butler County.

brief history and some interesting anecdotes noting the Third Kentucky laid claim to having "seen more active service in this country" than any other volunteer regiment. It reported;

> *"Since the day this regiment was called to go to defend the country until the present time the boys of the gallant Third have always been ready to respond to the call to go to the front. That they have met with disappointment is not the fault of the men comprising the regiment. Many of them fully expected to eat their Christmas dinner in Porto Rico, and at Newport News when the order was given to embark for foreign shores there was great rejoicing among them. Now that there is the prospect of being sent to Cuba the members of this regiment are feeling more cheerful...".*

The article noted the men did not like sitting around in camp and were

> *"anxious to make a reputation in the war which will make all Kentuckians feel proud of them. The officers are as eager as the enlisted men to see actual service, and have left nothing undone toward having this regiment among the first ordered to Cuban shores. Whether to Havana or Santiago, they are all ready and anxious to go."*

The regiment had an African-American civilian member named Romelius M. Garner, nicknamed 'Shorty'. He was a 32-yeard old dwarf, 42 inches tall weighing 42 pounds. According to the report, he was

> *"found on Snodgrass hill at Chickamauga one afternoon when some of the Company A boys were up there hunting rabbits. After receiving an invitation to join the regiment he agreed to go along as mascot if the boys would see that he had plenty to eat. 'Shorty' is one of the best poker players in the army, and sends home each month a neat sum...when 'the war is over' he intends to locate in Henderson, Ky., and open a boot blacking establishment."*

A raccoon named 'Dave' was a mascot. Described as fat and "most playful", it belonged to First Sergeant Louis A. Cramer of Company L. The animal was found as a baby and the soldiers fed it out of a bottle. As an older animal, it was described as

> *"very tame and hasn't any bad manners. He spends most of his time chained to a stake in front of the row of tents belonging to the band. Every day or so some of the boys take him down to the creek and let him hunt for crawfish. His playmate is 'Uno', a little yellow cur [dog]. They are fond of each other and roll around and around, having a good time generally."*

'Dave' became an attraction in camp. The report said,

> *"An enterprising young citizen was out to camp Saturday and took 'Dave's' picture. He seemed to be delighted and put his head on one side, looking very coquettish. 'Dave' is always glad to receive visitors, especially if they bring along any candy or [food]."*

On the night of November 5th the men organized a new veterans organization called 'The Service Men of the Spanish War' modeled on the Grand Army of the Republic. The camp in Lexington was named Henry Clay Camp No. 1 and Colonel Thomas J. Smith of the Third Kentucky helped draft the articles of incorporation.[80] This organization would unite with two other veteran groups in 1904 to become the United Spanish War Veterans.[81]

---

[80] *The San Francisco Call*, 'New Society of War Veterans: Is Patterned After the Grand Army', November 7, 1898, page 4; *The (Sacramento) Record-Union*, November 7, 1898, 'A New Society: The Service Men of the Spanish War Organized'.

[81] The United Spanish War Veterans (USWV) was born on April 18, 1904 when the three major Spanish War veterans groups united under one organization. These were the National Association of Spanish-American War Veterans, the National Army and Navy

On to Columbus

On Friday, November 11th the Third Kentucky began movement to Camp Conrad in Columbus, Georgia where they were to winter over.[82] The trip was fatal to two Third Kentucky soldiers when a section of the train separated and crashed partially demolishing one of the cars and seriously injuring Privates James A. Kindard, Company K and Walter Isnogal, Company I.[83] They died of their injuries. A black cook in the officer's mess, Lige Hathaway, attempted to board the train and fell under the cars where the rolling stock cut his legs off above the knees killing him. A Private Dunny of Company K also fell between two cars and his right leg was crushed so bad it had to be amputated.[84] A teamster identified as J.C. Starret also had a leg crushed during the rail trip.[85]

On the way to Georgia it was arranged for the regiment's train to stop in Bowling Green which was Colonel Smith's

---

Spanish War Veterans and the National Encampment of Service Men of the Spanish War. The latter was established in Lexington, Kentucky on November 5, 1898 and one of its main organizers was Colonel Thomas J. Smith of the Third Kentucky Infantry. In October 1906 the New England centered Legion of Spanish War Veterans incorporated under the umbrella of the USWV. In May 1908 the Veteran Army of the Philippines formally incorporated into the USWV. It died off as an organization when the last veteran passed away. The USWV lives in spirit through the Sons of Spanish-American War Veterans (SSAWV) and the Daughters of 98. For more information on the SSAWV visit: http://www.ssawv.org/

[82] *The (Maysville, Kentucky) Evening Bulletin*, 'Third Kentucky In Camp', page 1. They were brigaded with the 160th Indiana Volunteer Infantry and the 1st West Virginia Volunteer Infantry.

[83] These names do not correlate to individuals in the Third Kentucky roster. It is possible the names were misreported or existing records are incomplete.

[84] This was likely Private Arthur L. Dunn of Company K.

[85] *The (Maysville, Kentucky) Evening Bulletin*, November 15, 1898, 'Kentucky Boys Killed'. Starret is not listed on the roster and may have been a civilian contractor.

hometown. Lieutenant Bebout described this visit.

> *"One of our most pleasant experiences of our trip here, was a stop at Bowling Green, Ky., the home of Col. [T.J.] Smith [regimental commander]. We arrived there Saturday morning about ten o'clock and [spent] three hours in the town; a sumptuous dinner was served the boys by the citizens of that genuine Kentucky town. After dinner the regiment gave a parade through the town, which was witnessed by thousands of citizens."*[86]

At one point a private attempted to exit a railcar in violation of orders resulting in the soldier on guard duty to knock him down with the butt of his rifle.

The train continued to Montgomery by way of Nashville and Birmingham. In Nashville one of the black cooks from Company F had his legs cut off when he slipped and fell under the train while it was stopped.[87] At Montgomery the men changed trains to the Georgia and Alabama Railroad arriving in Columbus on Sunday night, November 13th. The men remained on the trains overnight and marched to the camp on the morning of November 14.

On Thanksgiving Day Lieutenant Lewis Bebout wrote in a letter home the cost of transporting the regiment from Lexington to Columbus was over $10,000. When the Kentuckians arrived, they were encamped with the 160th Indiana and were awaiting the First West Virginia to complete the brigade organization. In his letter, Bebout described the town of Columbus and shared some thoughts. He said Columbus was;

---

[86] *The Crittenden (Marion, Ky) Press*, December 1, 1898, 'Down In Georgia: A Member of the Third Kentucky Tells Something of Army Life'. Down in Georgia', letter dated November 24, 1898 from 2nd Lt. Lewis L. Bebout, 3rd Kentucky Infantry, U.S. Volunteers.
[87] *The Bee*, November 17, 1898, 'Third Kentucky',

"a peculiar old southern city, and about 50 years behind the age in which we live. The streets here are about twice as wide as Marion's [Ky] broadest thoroughfare and have rows of trees through the center of the streets. There is no sidewalk here. The population numbers 30,000; it is located on the banks of the Chattahoocie (sic) river; across the river is Phoenix City and Girard, Ala., towns of about 5,000 each. The towns are connected by bridge and have a street car system extending across the river. Our camp is located at the edge of Columbus, in what was, until we came, a large cotton field. Our first day was spent in pulling cotton stalks and preparing the ground for the camp. The soil is sandy and unfit for anything, even cotton. Our camp is surrounded by a nice growth of pines. A large field of cotton stands just to the west of our camp, and presents an appearance of a field of snow; it makes very pretty scenery. Since we have been here it has rained constantly, with the exception of the last four days; Sunday he 20th was the first sunny day we have had, in an hour after sunrise the camp was as dry as though it had not rained in a month.

"Soldiers being something new to the people here, a large crowd came out on that day to inspect the camp and witness dress parade. The city papers here estimated the crowd from ten to fifteen thousand. We have been treated very kindly by the citizens here, and most of the boys are very well pleased with the camp.

"There is not a great deal of difference in the climate here and at home. The nights are very chilly, really cold. Sunday was warm as a July day at home. Today is Thanksgiving day, and as I look down the company street and see the boys in different games, I feel that I really have something to be thankful for. We left Paducah on May 7th with 106 men in our company, all healthy, robust and manly fellows, who were able to stand the rigid medical examination which we were required to stand. We went to Lexington and were mustered into service; we arrived at Chickamauga on June 2nd; there we were subjected to hardships which I trust will never occur again to one of Uncle Sam's soldier.

Many of the boys became ill there from the exposure which necessarily attended our campaign. In July we left Chickamauga under orders to proceed to Newport News, Va, then to take transports for Porto Rico. We left some of our boys in the hospital at Chickamauga where one of them died; many went with us to Newport News who were really unfit for service, but were anxious to get to the front. When we left Newport News, to return to Lexington, we left nine men in the hospital there (our regiment left 300). Those of us who returned to Lexington, were not looking or feeling as we should like. I had lost 35 pounds from the time I left Paducah until I left Newport News. The other boys had lost about the same.

At Lexington we had an ideal camp, and within a week after we got there everyone felt better and began to look better, and this bright Thanksgiving day, I can truly say I am thankful our men are all in camp, and looking as well or better than they did on that bright May morning when they left their homes and loved ones in old Kentucky, full of hope, courage and patriotism, ready and anxious to do the bidding of their country.

"At headquarters all is activity making preparations for our departure for Cuba. We are under orders to be prepared to move on two hours' notice. From what knowledge I can gain I think we will not get away from here before the 10th or 15th of December."[88]

---

[88] Ibid, *The Crittenden (Marion, Ky) Press*, December 1, 1898, 'Down In Georgia'; Undated newspaper clipping from *The Crittenden (*Marion, KY) *Press*. Bebout mustered with the Marion company as an Orderly Sergeant in May and was promoted to First Sergeant. On October 7, 1898 he was elected to the positon of 2nd Lieutenant by the men of Company K. A report said, "Lieutenant Bebout was not only next in line for promotion, but is one of the most popular members of the company as well, and all the boys are glad to see his deserved promotion." See *Paducah Daily Sun*, October 8, 1898, page 4, 'LIEUT. BEBOUT: Mr. L.L. Bebout Elected Second Lieutenant of Company K';

Bebout was correct on the mid-December date for the movement to Cuba. First Army Corps General James H. Wilson noted in his memoir, "It was originally intended that the First Army Corps should reach the island in December, but lack of Army transports made it impossible to carry that intention into effect till early in January 1899."[89]

Camp illnesses continued to stress the regiment leading to some medical discharges. In November they had 108 new sick cases but Dr. Bell says these were mainly "those that are due to exposure to inclement weather, such as coryza, rheumatism, bronchitis, etc.". He wrote,

> *"venereal diseases, syphilis, chancroid and gonorrhea have been prevalent. We have recommended that all syphilitics be discharged. We have had no typhoid fever during this month. The cases on this report that are diagnosed typhoid fever are all convalescents. There had been no new cases of any contagious disease other than those mentioned above."*

Medical Conditions

There were only 27 persons remaining on sick report by the end of the month.[90] The Army Surgeon General later reassessed six of these cases as likely typhoid.

December saw 178 new medical cases. Dr. Bell reported most of the sick were afflicted with diseases "incident to exposure and damp weather" noting

> *"many cases of influenza have developed during the latter part of the month. The report includes many chronic cases. Discharges have been recommended for these. Two cases of measles have*

---

[89] James Harrison Wilson, <u>Under the Old Flag</u> (Westport, CT: Greenwood Press, Publishers) 1971. Volume II, p473.
[90] Third Kentucky Regiment, November 1898 Medical Report, quoted in <u>Typhoid Fever Report</u>, page 40-41

developed. These were sent to the brigade hospital and their clothing has been disinfected. All who have been exposed to these cases had previously had measles."

There were 42 sick cases still listed by the end of the month.[91] At least 16 of these cases were reassessed by the Surgeon General as typhoid giving the Third Kentucky a total of 219 probable typhoid cases for the year, many of which the Surgeon General claimed were not accurately diagnosed at the time. Dr. Bell objected to this post-war assessment stating "all cases of continued fever are classed as typhoidal in nature. This is taking much for granted." The Surgeon General's report indicated 17 men died of disease while in the Third Kentucky, eleven of these were from typhoid.[92]

Orders and Murder
On December 30, orders were received for General James H. Wilson, commanding the First Army Corps, to initiate movement to Matanzas Province, Cuba "to assist in maintaining good government there". The command consisted of the Third Kentucky Infantry, the Eighth Massachusetts Infantry, and the 160th Indiana Infantry. All were to be fully armed and equipped for field service and supplied with forage and 30 days rations.

On the night of January 7th, 1899 while the regiment was loading its quartermaster and commissary stores for transport to Savannah, there was an altercation between a Provost Guard Henry Denton of Company M and Robert Hoskins[93] of Company E, Third Kentucky. Denton's patrol area was on Fifth Avenue and Sixth Street which was described as the 'tenderloin district of the city'. Around 7:10 three shots were

---

[91] Third Kentucky Regiment, December 1898 Medical Report, quoted in <u>Typhoid Fever Report</u>, page 40-41
[92] <u>Typhoid Fever Report</u>, page 39-42, 159
[93] The news reports gave the name as 'Haskins' but it correlates to Private Hoskins.

fired in quick succession and persons heard a cry for help. According to reports,

> *"A woman named Nettie Witman ran to the door and saw young Denton lying on the pavement with his gun at his side. She approached him and heard him say: 'I am shot'. Other provost guards soon arrived and carried their wounded comrade into the house, where he died within thirty minutes."*[94]

Hoskins had fled the scene leaving behind his overcoat which was caught in a barbed wire fence. Tangled up, he slipped out of the coat and abandoned it. This lead to his identification.

Reportedly the provost guard had orders to arrest Hoskins "whenever he was seen in town." Denton observed Hoskins at about 7 p.m. "enter the house of ill-fame of Maude Miller and arrested him. As soon as he got his prisoner on the street Hoskins pulled a thirty-eight-caliber pistol and fired three shots, one of which was fatal."

A newspaper reported,

> *"After the killing Haskins came back to the regiment, turned his gun and effects over to the First Sergeant, and after donning a suit of citizen's clothes left for points unknown."*

Hoskins was believed to have fled to the mountains of Kentucky.[95] Within a week he was tracked to Albany, Georgia where he was identified to military authorities by Ellen Miller, a woman described by the press as a 'demi

---

[94] Denton was from Junction City, Boyle County, Kentucky and described as "one of the most efficient and popular men in the regiment." See the *Hartford (Ky) Herald*, January 11, 1899, page 2.
[95] Ibid, 'Henry Denton's Slayer'. Haskins was from Estill County, Kentucky; *The Spout Spring (Ky) Times*, January 14, 1899, 'Kentucky Newslets'

monde' and whom Hoskins had been with the night of the murder. Hoskins was arrested on January 15, 1899 and delivered to the Muscogee County jail in Columbus. He was "met by eight members of the provost guard, Capt. Feland in command, and was escorted to police headquarters, where trembling with fear, he begged piteously for protection." Hoskins was to be court-martialed and one officer reportedly told the press that "the man would be sentenced to be shot, as his crime appeared to be a most cold-blooded one."[96]

The Third Kentucky departed Columbus between 3:30 and 4:30 p.m. for Savannah on January 17 in three sections by way of the Central, the Georgia and Alabama and the Southern railroads. It was reported,

> *"As the regiment marched down Broad street, in front of the Rankin House, on the balcony of which stood Gen. Wiley and the officers of the division, the band struck up 'Dixie'. The first note was the signal for a rousing cheer, which came from the throats of the 3,500 men in line, as well as the spectators, who fairly thronged the sidewalks. As Color Sergeant Williams passed bearing the national flag another mighty shout went up. Williams is personally known to nearly every person in Columbus. 'Hurrah for the flag!' and 'Good bye, Williams!' were uttered in the same breath.*
>
> *"The men made a fine showing as they passed down Broad street. At the Union depot and the yards of the Southern road a vast throng assembled to tell the boys goodbye.*
>
> *"The officers of the Third Kentucky have been great social favorites, and for the nonce it seemed that society had adjourned in a body to the trains where its various members remained until the last coach pulled out. During the stay of the Kentuckians in*

---

[96] *The Hartford Journal,* January 18, 1899, page 3, 'Denton's Slayer Will Be Shot'. There was no report as to the outcome of his trial.

Columbus the regiment, as a body, has made more friends than any of the other regiments in the brigade. The regret at parting was mutual. The health of the regiment is good and the men went to Cuba well equipped for foreign service."[97]

---

[97] *The (Earlington, Ky) Bee*, January 19, 1899, 'Off to Savannah'.

Photographs

Colonel Thomas J. Smith, Commanding Officer of the Third Kentucky Infantry. He would later become the Mayor of Bowling Green.

Lt. Col. Jouett Henry (postwar)

Captain Ballard Trigg, Co. G

LOGAN FELAND (1869-1936) as a U.S. Marine Brigadier General. On mustering out as Captain of Company F, Third Kentucky Infantry in May 1899, Feland joined the Marines receiving a direct commission as a First Lieutenant. He served in the 'Banana Wars' and was a Lieutenant Colonel with the 5th Marine Regiment when it deployed to France in 1917 in World War I. He fought at **Chateau-Thierry** and commanded all troops in the **Belleau Wood** where his conspicuous gallantry would **earn** a Distinguished Service Cross. Promoted to full Colonel he commanded the regiment in subsequent battles. He was awarded four silver stars and retired as **a** Major General in 1933.

The Papers of William Thomas Taylor.

Among those serving in the Third Kentucky Infantry was North Carolina native William Thomas Taylor in Company A. He died in 1937 leaving several letters, photographs and other mementos of his service. These were donated for preservation by his grandchildren and have been published by the Sons of Spanish-American War Veterans as <u>The Papers of William Thomas Taylor</u>.

Breaking Camp in Columbus, Georgia *(Taylor Papers)*

BURIAL OF PRIVATE WILLIAM H. GRAHAM

Among William Thomas Taylor's papers was a small photo of a larger photo showing a group of men at the grave of Private William H. Graham, Co A, 3rd Kentucky Volunteer Infantry at La Union, Matanzas Province where they were stationed. Graham was killed by an accidental gunshot. There were notations on the photo enabling a full identification of the men pictured who appear to be the burial detail and firing squad, all likely friends of Graham. From left to right are Lt. Rice Ballard Trigg, Walter W. Wings, William W. Yates, W.E. Grundy, Cecil .P. Shacklett, Norman Hobgood, Fred L. Nightengale, Claude H. Basham, William Thomas Taylor and Clyde V. Craig. Lt. Trigg was from Company G while the remaining men were from Company A.

Company A Encampment at Union de Reyes, Cuba
(Taylor Papers)

Third Kentucky base of operations at
Castle San Severino, Matanzas, Cuba *(Taylor Papers)*

TRAINING – Eighth Massachusetts skirmish line in Cuba *(Taylor Papers)*

The battleship USS IOWA, Havana Harbor *(Taylor Papers)*

MAXIMO GOMEZ - The Commander of the Cuban Revolutionary forces was escorted by the Third Kentucky Infantry when he visited Matanzas in 1899.

Major General James H. Wilson

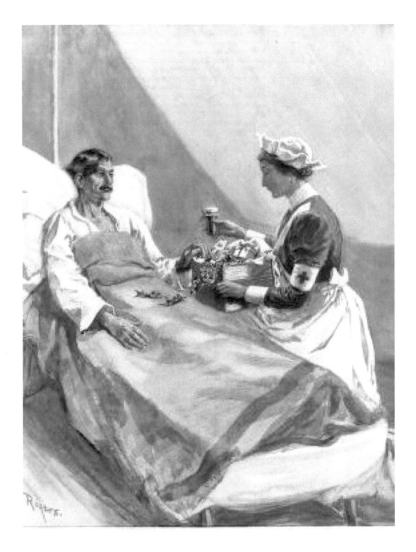

CIVILIAN NURSES - Civilian nurses were an integral part of the U.S. Army's medical system from training locations in the U.S. to forward locations in Cuba. Most were volunteers. Veterans recognized their service by allowing their membership in the United Spanish War Veterans.

Cuba and Matanzas Province

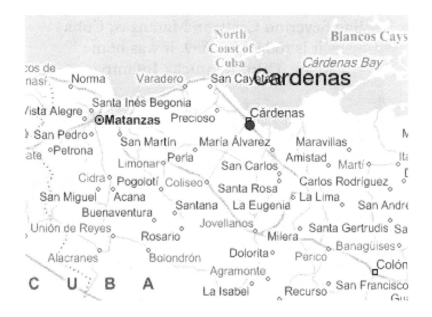

Third Kentucky Operations Area in Cuba

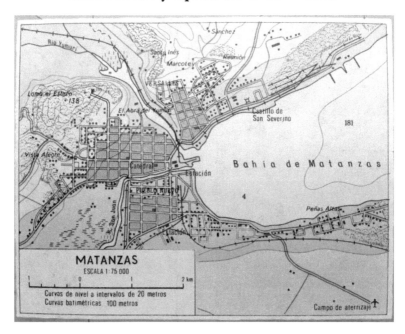

San Severino Castle in Matanzas, Cuba as it is today. In 1899, it was home to the Third Kentucky Infantry.

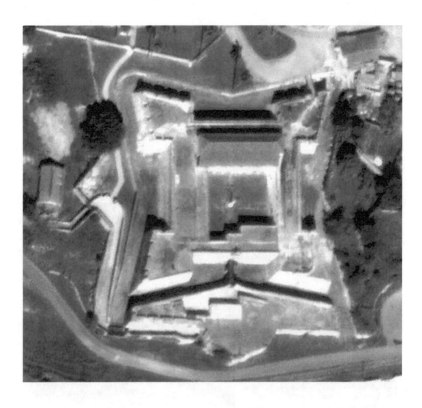

CUBAN CHILDREN - Refugees from a Spanish concentration center. *(Library of Congress)*

SPANISH SOLDIERS IN CUBA *(Library of Congress)*

CUBAN INSURGENTS *(Library of Congress)*

TARGET PRACTICE AT CAMP THOMAS *(Library of Congress)*

CAMP THOMAS, Georgia
(Photo from New Georgia Encyclopedia)

'THE BOULEVARD' – Camp Thomas Hospital Street
(U.S. National Library of Medicine Digital Collections)

DAUFUSKIE ISLAND DISINFECTING STATION – This is a close up of another image. It shows soldiers carrying bedrolls, knapsacks and equipment as the troops begin to disinfect their equipment during the quarantine period. *(Detroit Public Library Digital Image)*

CHAPTER 4

ON TO CUBA!

Wilson's First Army Corps set sail on January 7 with advance elements arriving in Matanzas on January 10. The men of the Third Kentucky embarked on the U.S. Army transport *Minnewaska* on January 18th, departing that night for Cuba. Only the sick and those to be discharged were left behind.[98]

Just before their departure, the officers of the Third Kentucky presented Kentucky Governor Bradley with a gift of two large "cut-glass water bottles and a dozen glasses of the same material, inclosed in a beautiful case, upon which is a silver plate containing the names of the regimental officers."[99]

There was also a last minute attempt by Congressman John Daniel Clardy, at the behest of his former colleague David Grant Colson, to have the Third Kentucky derailed and replaced by the Fourth Kentucky for which Colson served as Colonel. Colson was one of four members of the House of

---

[98] *Hopkinsville Kentuckian,* **January 20, 1899, 'Off For Cuba', page4.**
[99] *The (Stanford, Ky) Semi-Weekly Interior,* **January 10, 1899, page 3.**

Representatives that went into uniform for the war. It was determined that, as a result of Constitutional requirements, all four men effectively resigned their seats and could not be reseated. With the demobilization of the Fourth Kentucky, Colson was out of a job and tried to use political influence to keep the Fourth on duty so he could remain on active service. Congressman Clardy personally visited the Assistant Secretary of War to try to help his friend. The War Department reportedly notified Congressman Clardy, "Too late, the Third is the better of the two."[100]

Lieutenant Lewis L. Bebout, Company K, briefly described the trip to Cuba. He noted the unit departed Savannah on Wednesday night, January 18th and arrived at Matanzas on Saturday January 21. He said the voyage "was one of the most pleasant trips I ever made. The weather was fine and our vessel was as smooth as an Ohio river boat." He described the ship to the folks at home;

> *"The trip was a grand one. Sunrise and sunset on the waters is a beautiful picture to behold. The transport we came on— Minnewaska, is considered the finest transport in the service, and she is certainly a model, being 485 feet long, 65 feet wide and 43 feet in depth so you can see she is quite a large vessel. The men all had quarters in the "hold" and had plenty of room. There being room for 3500 men, instead of one regiment.*[101]

Another Third Kentucky soldier made note of the seasickness. He wrote,

> *"We left Columbus, Ga., on the 17th and landed in Savannah on the 18th, and started across the Big Pond that night on the*

---

[100] *Hartford (Ky) Republican*, January 20, 1899, 'Off For Cuba, page 2.
[101] *The (Marion, KY) Crittenden Press*, February 9, 1899, 'From Cuba, Lt. Bebout Writes About his Trip and the Country', page 1.

> *Transport [Minnewaska]. The first day out was nice, the sea being as nice as could be expected. The second day being a little monotonous, for everywhere we looked we could see nothing but water. We passed the Florida Keys the second day, and struck out across the Straits for Matanzas, arriving there about 7 o'clock on the morning of the 21st. Everybody enjoyed the trip immensely, there being not much seasickness, only a few got sick, and I was one of the few. If any of you were ever sea sick, you know how we felt. We were too sick to eat, and when a soldier gets too sick to eat, he certainly is bad off."*[102]

Lt. S.F. South described the seasickness in greater detail recalling the steamer "rode the waves as gracefully as a duck, though our second night the Captain told us there were indications of a storm." They ship hit the storm about midnight, he said adding,

> *"I did not get sea-sick a bit, but some of the soldier boys tried to see how near they could empty their stomachs for breakfast. The horses and mules could not keep on their feet and the waves rolled mountain high. We were scared, though the crew said we were in no danger at all…I can tell you that a storm on the ocean is calculated to take all the courage out of a greenhorn like us, and yet the sight of a storm at midnight on the sea is a grand one, and is well worth the uneasiness it causes, especially when in a helpless condition, while enduring its awful power. I will never forget it as long as I live, should that be a hundred years."*[103]

Lt. South said the following day was "a typical tropical one" and the men of the regiment, most of whom had never seen the ocean before joining the Army, spent the day on deck on the lookout for other ships and watching ocean life. He

---

[102] *The Hickman Courier,* March 10, 1899, 'Hickman Boy In Cuba: the Country, Social Conditions, &c'. Letter from Jim Robertson, Co. K, Third Kentucky Volunteer Infantry, USV.
[103] *Frankfort (Ky) Roundabout,* February 25, 1899, 'Letter from Cuba', Lt. S.F. South, Co. H, Third Kentucky Volunteer Infantry.

wrote home,

> "We found great sport whenever we struck a school of porpoise. The large, but harmless, monsters would jump eight and ten feet out of the water and all seem to [be] coming toward the vessel, and would continue to follow for miles. Another novel sight was the flying fish. It would rise out of the water and fly for several yards and then back to the deep blue sea again. And the strangest of all to me was the fact that you could go from one side of the vessel to the other, from the fo'castle to the stern, and, although the day was very bright, and not a cloud to obscure the vision, as far as the eye could reach there was nothing but the bluest water."[104]

Rochester Wallingford also detailed the unit's sea movement in a January 23 letter home from Matanzas. He wrote;

> "We broke Camp at Columbus last Tuesday morning, and reached Savanah, Ga., Wednesday morning, and boarded Minnewaska at 8 o'clock that night, and at 11 o'clock the prow of our vessel turn towards Cuba, and for the first time in life I was on the "briney deep" and to tell the truth I was proud of it. We were out of sight of land two days, and a good many of the boys were seasick, but I stood it comfortably as an 'old tar'. Our ship was 487 feet long, and it seemed to me that as much could be stored away on her as in the whole town of Marion. While coming we saw all kinds of ships and all kinds of fish in the ocean."[105]

At one point in the trip, through a misunderstanding of some sort, the entire Regiment was "called to quarters" one afternoon about two o'clock for the purpose of being subjected to a salt-water bath from a hose. While in quarters

---

[104] Ibid, Lt. South Letter
[105] *The Critenden (Ky) Press*, February 2, 1899, 'At Matanzas: A Crittenden Boy Writes From Cuba'.

they were ordered to strip, with Company A in the lead, and procced to the top deck where they would be sprayed down. When the order was issued, Company A refused and was cheered on by Company G. Captain Burchfield of Company A reportedly threatened the troops and "ordered one man under arrest, but the men refused to obey the orders."

Captain Bailey, a former Baptist minister, offered to strip and lead the men "to the obnoxious bath". Nobody moved, all the men considering the order an "outrage". Every other Company captain had the same result when word circulated the hatches would be closed off and hoses placed below decks to spray the men in their quarters. This incited more anger and "a rush was made for the upper deck." In the meantime the 'mutiny' had been reported to Colonel Smith and he appeared as the men were rushing for the upper decks. Colonel Smith stated "he had not given any order for the hose bath. He called up the band and music quieted the troubled spirits of the men"[106]

---

[106] *The (Washington) Times*, February 4, 1899, 'Declined Hose Bath: An Amusing Incident on the Transport Minnewaska'

Sidebar: The Foundation for Intervention

Spanish Concentration Camps

The Cuban Revolution against Spain began in earnest in 1895. In 1896 Spain dispatched General Valeriano Weyler to Cuba to quell the insurrection. He declared martial law and established a policy of 'reconcentrado', creating camps to relocate -- or reconcentrate -- rural citizens, feasibly under the protection of the Spanish Army, as a way to deny food and other support to the rebels. Over 800,000 rural citizens were in various camps by March 1898.

While the intent had been to keep the citizens alive, the rural agricultural system broke down. The reconcentration policy took the workers from the fields and put them in camps by the cities. Food shortages, lack of camp sanitation and lack of medicines led to starvation, disease and death. Spain reported 225,000 died by late March 1898 and the Red Cross reported as many as 435,000 the same time.[107] Reportedly 25%-30% of the Cuban citizenry died. U.S. diplomats and newspapers reported on these events which earned Weyler the nickname of 'Butcher'. Reports of the atrocities incited the American people and laid the foundation of support for American military intervention.

On March 14, 1898 it was reported that 20,000 people had

---

[107] *Baltimore Sun*, **March 24, 1898, 'Horrors of Cuban War'**

died in Matanzas in the past year to include 550 in the first two weeks of March. The American Consul reported 10,000 were known to be starving to death in Matanzas alone with an average of 43 dying each day.[108] This situation had not been substantially resolved by the time the Third Kentucky Infantry arrived in Cuba in January 1899.

WHY WE FOUGHT – From the Photographic <u>History of the Spanish-American War</u> (New York: Pearson Co.) 1898. The caption stated, in part:

> *"Soon after the outbreak of the Cuban revolution in 1895, reports began to reach the United States of acts of cruelty perpetrated by the Spanish. Captured rebels were not the only sufferers. Their portion was death and solitary confinement, and non-combatants accused of sympathizing with the insurrection fared little better.*

---

[108] *Baltimore Sun,* March 13, 1898, 'A City of Horrors'

These unwarranted acts were boldly asserted by American newspaper correspondents but vigorously denied by the Spanish officials...In any event isolated cases, though clearly proved, hardly seemed to warrant so grave a step as armed intervention... Finally, however, General Weyler issued his famous edict of concentration 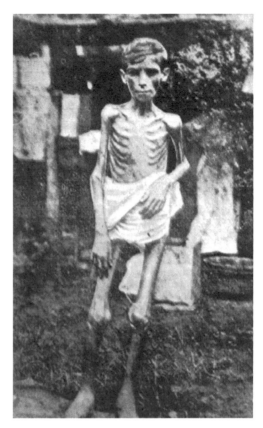 *whereby non-combatants were driven in from the country and made to stay in the fortified towns...they were without means of sustaining themselves and many died from starvation and disease...Even then, many weeks elapsed before the true state of affairs became generally known...Finally, however, several Senators and Congressmen paid personal visits to the points where the policy of concentration had been carried into effect, and these witnesses...brought back word that the stories of the suffering and starvation of helpless old men, women and children had not been even half told. Actual photographs similar to the one above were also shown. The people and Congress were finally aroused. An ultimatum was delivered to Spain, and on its rejection a formal declaration of war followed on April 25, 1898."*

General James H. Wilson, military governor of Matanzas, in making a survey of the entire province in early 1899 wrote,

> *"...it was evident that starvation had been abroad in the land and that if the conditions existing at the close of the war with Spain had continued a few months longer half the population would have been dead from starvation. In other words, Weyler's policy of reconcentration with its manifold horrors was everywhere doing its fatal work, and, had our intervention not put an end to it, there can be but little doubt that a year's further enforcement of it would have destroyed the bulk of the Cuban population."*[109]

---

[109] Ibid, Wilson, p.485.

CHAPTER 5

OCCUPATION DUTY

The original U.S. mission in occupying Cuba was to ensure "pacification" and then leave. Due to the Teller Amendment the U.S. would not exercise sovereignty or control except in regards to pacifying hostile forces..

On January 1, 1899 General John R. Brooke, the military governor and head of the U.S. Army of Occupation issued an order stating he was the representative of the President of the United States and charged with "putting an end to the distressing conditions on the island" through a military government which would provide protection to the people and their property, encourage a return to civil pursuits, and facilitate commercial traffic by leveraging existing civil administrators.[110] There were no implementation guidelines for subordinates however leading each commander to "make

---

[110] Ibid, Wilson, p476-479. General Wilson was critical of this order because it said nothing of recognizing Cuban independence or the insurgent Republican government while allowing the Spanish government infrastructure to remain in place. He felt the wording left open the impression the U.S. intended to remain indefinitely. Cuban independence would eventually be recognized in 1902.

it up" as things progressed. General Wilson complained that there was no detailed mission guidance recalling, "We were left absolutely to our own conception of the situation and what it required of us."[111]

Records and reports from the period suggest the American occupation duty in Cuba evolved into several missions. These included supporting civil administration, overseeing the safe repatriation of Spanish soldiers (there were an estimated 15,000 to 20,000 in Matanzas[112]), overseeing the demobilization of Cuban rebel soldiers and transitioning them back to civilian labors, the formation and training of a regional police force and civil affairs work that included distribution of a relief fund and food to people in various communities starving because of the wartime disruption of agricultural foodstuffs.

The Spanish Depart Matanzas

General Wilson noted he and his troops arrived in Matanzas "two days before the last Spanish troops embarked for home." He wrote, "Without recognizing the insurgents or having anything to do with the insurgent leaders, the Spaniards had maintained order and drawn in their detachments as rapidly as transports could be furnished to take them out of the country."

The Spanish forces remained east of the bay in Matanzas

---

[111] Ibid, Wilson, p483.
[112] War Department. Annual Report of the Secretary of War. *Report of the Chief of Engineers, Part 1* (Washington: Government Printing Office) 1901. See Captain (Lt Col, USV) Edgar Jadwin diary, page 9. He estimates 15,000 to 20,000 Spanish troops still present and he commanded the Third Battalion, USV Engineers accepting formal transfer of the province from Spain on January 1, 1899. See also Major John Biddle, Chief Engineer, U.S. Volunteers noted "There were 15,000 to 20,000 Spanish soldiers in the city, assembled from different towns in the province."

while the Americans occupied the western part and Fort San Severino. Wilson wrote,

> *"No prescribed ceremonies or courtesies took place between the Spanish and American forces. Our communications were of the most formal character and there was no sign of the departing sovereignty of Spain or the oncoming possession of the United States, except that at noon, when, with appropriate salutes, the Spanish colors were lowered and the Stars and Stripes were hoisted to the head of the flagstaff in San Severino. That night the last transport disappeared, and for the first time [Cuban Insurgent] General Betancourt and his native troops made their appearance, but not till after I sent a courier to the country to find the General and his escort and bring them into the city for a patriotic fiesta."*[113]

General Wilson embraced the Cuban insurgent commander and welcomed him and his troops into the city but stipulated the troops should not enter the town with ammunition nor would they be allowed to harass or provoke the Spaniards remaining in town. Wilson said the welcoming initiated a positive relationship with Betancourt and between the Cuban insurgents and the U.S. Army[114]

Before leaving Cuba the Spanish government created an autonomous government and appointed governors, mayors and town councils to ensure an orderly transition. General Wilson wrote,

> *"As far as I knew then or afterward, these officials were insulars of good character, conservative views, and fair education. In my province [Matanzas] they gave ready and cheerful support to the military government without putting themselves forward, claiming*

---

[113] Ibid, Wilson, p473-474.
[114] Ibid, Wilson, p474-475.

precedence, or pressing their views upon my attention.".[115]

The U.S. authorities helped establish civil order by allowing the previous Spanish government officials to continue in their offices though the U.S. did eliminate the special privileges of the Catholic Church in an effort to foster the freedom of all religions. The Spanish government positions were eventually transitioned to Cubans. [116]

How much of this work the Third Kentucky actually engaged in is not determined. Several officers were detached to support the Army administration from feeding the poor to guarding civil prisoners. Records suggest the regiment's primary value was its mere presence as it ensured security and the maintenance of a safe and stable environment as the various socio-economic changes occurred.[117]

Civil Affairs Work

The U.S. Army and Navy played an important role in stabilizing Cuba during the occupation period through civil affairs work. The Cuban rebellion had been underway since 1895. The combination of the Cuban rebel destruction of crops to keep them from feeding the Spanish and the Spanish reconcentrado program, where the people of the country were concentrated in camps to keep them from supporting the Cuban rebels, had a devastating effect on the agricultural base of the economy leading to a food shortage. The government of the United States stepped in to help feed the former reconcentrado prisoners and the poor of the various provinces. They also created jobs for local labor to help build the infrastructure.

---

[115] Ibid, Wilson, p475
[116] Ibid, Wilson, p475, 479
[117] *Rock Island Argus*, April 8, 1899, 'Will Reinstate General Gomez', page 1.

Local citizens were employed by the U.S. military authorities in constructing water lines for military camps, constructing railroad spurs to military camps and establishing supply depots, many of the latter constructed for the storage and later redistribution of food rations to Cuba's impoverished population.

Captain Noel Gaines of the Third Kentucky was detached from the regiment to oversee this work in Havana reportedly distributing 220,000 rations from 11 January to 2 February 1899. A news report indicated Captain Gaines had five districts to service. It noted,

> *"In the center of each district a depot has been established and provisions are issued to the poor every day. The soldiers who are detailed to this work are kept busy from opening to closing hours…".*[118]

Gaines expended $1,848.13 from February 15 to April 30 of which $1,544.68 was spent on Cuban relief and the remainder on expenses associated with running his office.[119]

The U.S. Army Commissary General identified the Mayors of outlying villages and whenever there was a request, the food would be issued and transported to the village for redistribution. Depots were established at Marianao, Pinar del Rio, Santiago, Cienfuegos, Matanzas and Trinidad. One

---

[118] *The Richmond (Va) Dispatch*, Feb 7, 1899, 'Feeding the Cubans: The Work No Being Carried On Systematically'.
[119] **Committee on Relations with Cuba, U.S. Senate.** *Letter of the Secretary of War Submitting A Consolidated Statement of Fiscal Affairs In the Island of Cuba, Under the United States Military Government, from January 1, 1899 to April 30, 1900.* **As Audited.** Division of Customs and Insular Affairs. December 13, 1900. (Washington, DC: Government Printing Office) 1900. **Disbursements Made By Capt. Noel Gaines, Third Kentucky Volunteers, disbursing officer at Habana'**, page 5-6.

report described the size of the ration as a "banquet" compared to what the people received in the internment camps. The normal ration consisted of one pound of cornmeal, 12 pounds of flour, two pounds of canned meat, two pounds of bacon, 90 pounds of coffee, 10 pounds of sugar, one to 50 liters of vinegar, 25 liters of pepper, 25 liters of salt, 15 pounds of rice and 25 liters of soap.[120] It is not reported how long these rations were expected to last before one could replenish supplies.

Private foundations also pitched in to help Cuba recover. The Cuban Industrial Relief Fund, which was later fully endorsed by the U.S. and Cuban governments, was established in November of 1898 and solicited donations enabling it to rent land for agriculture. Their plan was to equip farms and pay wages to day laborers "gradually enabling them to prepare to go to work on their own farms" with oxen, seeds and farm tools to be loaned for their use and paid for after the crops were harvested and sold.[121] Mrs. E. Grace Freer, one member of the organization, wrote of the plight of the widows and orphans, highlighting the situation in Matanzas where the Third Kentucky was stationed. She said,

> *"the greatest weight of suffering has fallen upon the helpless*

---

[120] Ibid, Feb. 7, 1899.

[121] **Education, A Monthly Magazine Devoted to the Science, Art, Philosophy and Literature of Education, *'The Cuban Industrial Relief Fund'* by Horace F. Barnes, Financial Director, Boston, Volume 19 (September 1898-June 1899), p369,, (Boston: Kasson & Palmer) 1899. The article says, "The Movement is wide apart from ordinary unconditional charity. It proposes to enable the great agricultural classes of Cuba to help themselves. They prefer this method of help, for the farmers are an industrious and frugal class. There are about 100,000 small farms in Cuba, yet nearly all of the farmers are homeless, penniless and starving. They only ask the loan of oxen, plows, hoes and seed, and their fertile soil will do the rest."**

women and children...for a woman to be homeless and destitute means misery and that leads to despair and death. One hundred and fifty thousand orphans today roam through this country, half-starved, like stray cats and dogs looking for scraps of food to keep their little bodies and souls together..."[122]

General Wilson reported 12,000 widows and 22,000 orphans in that province.[123] But it was not only the poor peasants who were destitute. Mrs. Freer observed that Cuba's former middle-class were also suffering. She said,

"There are thousands of women and children too proud to ask for help, too sensitive to receive public alms, yet waging a daily battle with hunger and despair. A striking instance of this fact was brought to light recently by an American Army officer who had been detailed to investigate the public schools of the city of Matanzas...During his investigation of the schools he took occasion to take a number of small children aside, one by one, and question them concerning their home life. These children were not of the reconcentrado class. Their families had never been in the charitably aided class. They were of well-to-do middle class, supposed to be above want. It was with the utmost difficulty that the officer could get the children to admit that they were hungry. They seemed to him to have 'something of the stoicism of our Indians and the non-resistance and fatalism of the East Indian'."[124]

---

[122] *New York Daily Tribune*, May 7, 1899, 'Some of Cuba's Women: The Conditions of Orphans and Widows In That Island', page 5.
[123] *Report of General James H. Wilson to the Adjutant General of the Army, 14 August 1899, Headquarters Department of Matanzas.* Contained in the *Annual Report of Brigadier General James H. Wilson, U.S.V., Commanding the Department of Matanzas and Santa Clara to Which Is Appended Special Report on the Industrial, Economic and Social Conditions Existing in the Department at the Date of American Occupation, and at the Present Time. Matanzas, Cuba, August 1st – September 7th, 1899.*
[124] Ibid.

The American officer shared his notes which described multiple instances of what he heard from the children in Matanzas. He said,

"An intelligent little mulatto girl, ten years old, usually had a cup of coffee in the morning and one meal a day, generally at 4 p.m. This was a common case. The meal usually consisted of rice and potatoes.

"A pretty little boy, five years old, gave his usual daily allowance as follows: a cup of coffee only at 8 a.m.; a dish of rice at 10 a.m.; rice and potatoes at 4 p.m. He had not eaten meat in a long time.

"A boy of fourteen had coffee today, but not every day; at 10 a.m. bread and rice cooked with lard; dinner at 4 p.m. of codfish and potatoes. This boy had had no meat in a year.

"A beautiful little girl, ten years old; coffee only at 7 a.m.; breakfast at 11 a.m. sometimes, but not very often; dinner yesterday of black beans and rice; sometimes no dinner at all, but gets something to eat every day; has had very little fresh meat, a small piece three weeks ago as a present. This child's father is dead.

"A girl, twelve years old; had no coffee this morning; may get breakfast, may not; breakfast, when there is any, of rice and codfish; dinner doubtful, but generally gets one meal a day. The father being sick, the family will be compelled to draw rations from the Americans.

"A girl, thirteen years old; father out of work; has coffee sometimes; never has breakfast; family have dinner when they can get it; child manages to get something to eat every day; is hungry now; been in the same condition since the war began; an intelligent child.

> *"A girl, thirteen years old, very intelligent; had coffee at 7:30 a.m. at her cousin's house because there was none at home; father a cobbler, sick in bed; had breakfast yesterday of bread and oil; dinner yesterday of bread and rice; sometimes has a sweet potato; some days has no food, but generally gets a little. This girl reluctantly admits that she sometimes is hungry.*
>
> *"A girl, twelve years old; very bad color; has no father; had coffee only, 8:30 a.m.; had breakfast yesterday of rice and pig's skin which a neighbor gave to her mother; dinner, generally at night, of rice, white beans, bread and coffee; has often had no food except bread and coffee at night.*
>
> *"A girl, nine years old, very intelligent and pretty; has coffee only, generally at 8 a.m.; family has only one meal a day, usually in the afternoon; when they have nothing they go to bed; when the father, who is a cobbler, has no work there is no food; sometimes they get two meals a day.*
>
> *"A girl, twelve years of age; intelligent, stout and strong-looking; at 10 a.m. had coffee only; nothing earlier; yesterday had no breakfast; yesterday had dinner at 2 p.m., rice soup only, the usual food; had fresh meat one day two weeks ago; sometimes has no food all day except coffee. The child's mother is a seamstress."*[125]

"If this is the life led by the children of the self-supporting class of Cubans in Matanzas, what can be the lot of the very poor?" Mrs. Freer asked, adding,

> *"The imagination fails to conceive of any one living on less. They country districts were swept bare of farmhouses and inhabitants by [former Spanish Governor Valeriano] Weyler's infamous order of concentration. Nothing was left which could sustain life. The country people were crowded into the towns and cities, where*

---

[125] **Ibid.**

nearly half a million died of starvation and disease.

"The survivors are still there, receiving an occasional dole of United States Army rations. They are unable to return to their homes, because they have only empty hands with which to rebuild their burned houses. They cannot resume the cultivation of their idle fields because they are literally beggars, without oxen, agricultural implements, seeds or domestic supplies with which to work. The American Government has done nothing to help the Cuban farmers. It has given them Army rations, but it has no legal means of providing them with oxen, tools and seeds. It has attempted to do no more than keep them alive until private philanthropy enables them to take care of themselves…there is just one way of permanently redeeming Cuba from its present condition of destitution and suffering. That way is not to give the people free soup and old clothes until they become hopelessly pauperized, but to give them work. The plan of the Cuban Industrial Relief Fund is to help the poor to help themselves."[126]

Mrs. Freer established a strong case for private philanthropy and noted "the civil and military governors of the Province of Matanzas assert that the need for the work is greater in Matanzas than in the Province of Havana. Major General Wilson has telegraphed that there are twenty-thousand starving people in Matanzas."

General Wilson also made the case for providing farmers with support to get them back on their feet. Import duties were going into the Cuban Insular Treasury administered by U.S. authorities, and was being used by authorities to construct road and rail infrastructure and government buildings. General Wilson noted this was useless until there

---

[126] **Ibid. Mrs. Freer's organization also had a system where they could place orphans in the homes of good Cuban families rather than by constructing "costly" new orphanages which would have required sustained funding for food and staff.**

were products to carry to market and that the monies should be used as loans to farmers so they could purchase animals, wagons and farm implements.[127] This situation would not get resolved by the time the Third Kentucky left Cuba and was one of the U.S. policies that were discussed over many months. Over $1.5 million would be expended on hospitals, charities, relief, and internal improvements.[128]

By February 1900 the industrial and political conditions of the country had improved dramatically under the combination of U.S. administration and philanthropic endeavors such as those offered by the Cuban Industrial Relief Fund. The success was such that the latter voted to cease the solicitation of funds and to propose dissolving.[129]

In regards to general security, the American concept was that the Cubans would pacify the island themselves. Cuban General Maximo Gomez, who had been ill and was getting treatment in the U.S., declared he would return to Cuba and help "pacify" the island from a small number regional bandits loosed by the war. U.S. Special Envoy Robert P. Porter welcomed the news noting,

> *"the advantage thus gained should be followed up by the American authorities. The entire policing of the island should be done by the Cubans themselves. The real wok is, in fact, now in the hands of Cuban soldiers, and law and order are well maintained. There should not be a moment's delay in the*

---

[127] *The (Washington) Times*, July 15, 1899, 'The Needs of Matanzas: General Wilson and Senor Betancourt Express Their Views'.
[128] Ibid, *A Consolidated Statement of Fiscal Affairs In the Island of Cuba*,
[129] New Outlook, Volume 64, February 3, 1900, 'The Cuban Industrial Relief Fund', page 247. Other organizations were also involved in drives to collect relief supplies that were sent to Cuba.

organization and equipment of these civil guards."[130]

General Gomez wrote to President McKinley, "The younger officers on both sides should come together and evolve preliminary policing plans and get those into working order without delay. Once this is well done matters will take care of themselves in Cuba."[131]

It was further determined by U.S. authorities that a minimal U.S. presence could support the Cuban police. General Wilson advocated a policy that allowed towns to hire their own police instead of having an overarching rural guard. He argued this would allow civil administrators in towns or localities to control the law enforcement arm thereby ensuring they were responsible to the people. Further the local police would also be subject to U.S. military inspections and oversight. Wilson said this policy was adopted and worked well.[132]

Because a smaller number of troops satisfy occupation requirements, the United States government decided to redeploy unneeded U.S. Army forces back to the U.S.

Third Kentucky in Matanzas
Cuba proved to be new and exciting to the men of the Third Kentucky who took the opportunity to write home of what they saw describing the culture, the environment and some of their challenges.

Lieutenant Lewis L. Bebout, Company K, detailed in a letter home the Third Kentucky's arrival at their encampment at Matanzas. He said,

---

[130] *Rock Island Argus*, February 4, 1899, 'Thing to Do in Cuba: According to the Opinion of Porter, the Special Envoy to Gen. Gomez', page 2
[131] **Ibid.**
[132] **Ibid, Wilson, 489.**

"We disembarked and went into a temporary camp, using our shelter tents (which are about the size of an umbrella). Our regiment will be divided up here into battalions and sent to different points. Our battalion, the first, goes to Union (oon-yon), the second goes to Cardenas. Our battalion will leave here at 1 o'clock today. Our place is about 35 miles in the interior, but they have a railroad there and we will not have to march the distance. This is well for the climate here is "hot" with a capital H, being about 100 in the shade.

"The day we got here was the beginning of a three days jubilee with the natives, and 20,000 Cuban soldiers were in the city to take part in it, and they had a big time. This people are indeed a "queer set" and the laziest fellows you ever saw, too lazy to move. They are all colors, no color line being drawn, they all associate together. Of course we cannot understand their language and their jabbering runs me about two-thirds crazy. I get mad when I see a right black fellow (who looks like a negro) and can't understand him, for they look natural and it seems could talk with us.

"I took a walk upon the mountain back of the city Sunday (taking most of my company with me) sightseeing, and just over the mountain west of the city is a valley about four miles in width and extending as far up the island as you can see. In this valley growing in abundance and wild, we found oranges, lemons, bananas, pine apples, cocoanuts, figs, dates, etc., and the sight is one that can not (sic) be described on paper, and once of the most beautiful I ever witnessed.

"And now a word about the people. The sights you see is appalling. Thousands of the reconcentrados are half-starved and too weak to walk much less work, and if any man has had any

doubt as to the barbarity of the Spaniards in their treatment of this people, it would all disappear upon sight of these unfortunate beings, and none of the boys regret anything they have done for them. They certainly present a pitiful appearance.

"I have had plenty to do since I landed on the Island, as I am in command of the company, both Captain [Britton B.] Davis and Lt. [Alfred D.] Stewart having been left in the states sick. We have two men in the hospital. It is very hard to get the boys to be careful of what they eat and drink; many eat too much fruit and drink too much water.[133]

"We are camped at present in a place where it is so rocky you can't find dirt enough to drive a tent pin. When we move we hope to be better located. These rocks are full of centipedes, tarantulas and snakes, and several of the boys have been bitten. The boys roll up in a blanket and go to sleep, and wake up with a centipede in their bed for a bed fellow."[134]

Company K's Jim Robertson described Matanzas as a:

"city of 40,000 but you would not think so, it covers such a small space of ground as compared to an American city of that size. It is a very dirty city, but the government is having it cleaned up as fast as possible, preparing for the hot season. The streets are not over 25 feet wide and the side walks are so narrow that two cannot walk side by side on them.

"It is a very hard matter to tell the residences from the business houses, as all the houses are built up to the side walk, a yard being a thing unseen. All the houses have bars over the windows,

---

[133] Lt. South mentioned the area was "rich in tropical trees, plants and fruits, such as cocoanut trees, lemon, lime and orange. The cocoanut trees have no fruit, though the lemon and orange trees are full and the second crop of bananas are on the plants. The fig and date trees have fruit on them in abundance, and you can buy more fruit for a cingo centime, or five cents, than you can eat."
[134] *The (Marion, KY) Crittenden Press*, February 9, 1899, 'From Cuba, Lt. Bebout Writes About his Trip and the Country', page 1.

and anyone that can afford a carriage invariably has it setting in the hallway. The Lord knows what they do with the horses, either put them on the roof or in the cellar."[135]

Rochester Wallingford also detailed the unit's movement in a January 23 letter home from Matanzas. He wrote;

"This is a nice country over here, and I like it very much. I wish you could see how the Cubans live. Their houses have no chimneys, and there are iron bars across the windows and doors, reminding one of a jail. They dress in all styles, and some don't dress much any way. Of course there are many nice people here, some of them well to do, and the boys and girls ride horse-back a great deal. The Cubans come out to camp, and pick up the old scraps of bread and meatskins, and carry them home to eat, and some glad to get them.

"Our regiment is just back from town. I went into the old fort yesterday, and saw the place where the Spaniards executed Cubans. They blindfolded and then shot them.

"John Nunn is still in Columbus, he was getting all right when I saw him last. I never was in better health nor enjoyed myself more."[136]

Lt South also gave a detailed account of Matanzas. He wrote,

"Some of the buildings are perfect palaces, especially the suburban residences and public buildings, although all of them have a prison like appearance on account of the iron grating before all the doors and windows. The windows reach from floor to ceiling, and

---

[135] ***The Hickman Courier,*** **March 10, 1899, 'Hickman Boy In Cuba: the Country, Social Conditions, &c'. Letter from Jim Robertson, Co. K, Third Kentucky Volunteer Infantry, USV; Ibid, Lt. South Letter. He said Matanzas had a population of 75,000.**
[136] ***The Crittenden (Ky) Press,*** **February 2, 1899, 'At Matanzas: A Crittenden Boy Writes From Cuba'.**

not a one that I have been able to see have a pane of glass in them. The streets are very narrow and irregular, so that two can scarcely walk side by side...on the whole the city makes one think they are living three or four hundred years ago. Yes, even thousands, and walking through some old place mentioned in the Good Book, or some ancient history."[137]

He wrote of the encampment between the old Spanish forts on the outskirts of the city which overlooked Matanzas Bay. He said,

"My tent, at one time, was pitched against the wall, beside which, only a short time ago, hundreds of Cuban patriots were lined up and slaughtered like so many cattle by the hated Spaniards. You can see the bullet holes on its rugged sides were the men were forced to stand to be shot down. I have picked several bullets from the wall and one little dark-eyed fellow showed me the exact spot where his father stood when shot, and where he was made to stand and watch it. The marksman missed his aim, and at once his head was cut off."[138]

Cuban Rebels Awaiting Execution *(National Archives)*

---

[137] Ibid, Lt. South Letter.
[138] Ibid, Lt. South Letter

Cuban Critters

The native wildlife and insects also figure in many letters, particularly the centipedes which had a poisonous venom. While it is not always deadly to humans, the bites are painful, anywhere from the feeling of a bee sting to something worse. It causes swelling around the bite, itching and could cause a reaction resulting in headaches, nausea, sweating and swelling of lymph nodes. For younger people, older people and people with weak hearts, the bites can be deadly. Lt. South mentioned several of the men in the Third Kentucky "had been bitten by tarantulas and stung by centipedes. The bites make an awful looking arm and limbs and is very painful, but as yet there have been no deaths from them."

One of the regimental surgeons noted the presence of insects writing,

> *"I found a centipede, about five inches long, in my shoe the other morning when I put it on. It did not bite me, and I afterwards killed it. A number of the boys have been bitten by different things; but none of them have been very serious. Little lizards, or some reptile of that species, are about as common as grasshoppers at home. You can see them hurrying and scurrying around the rocks."*[139]

At least one soldier determined to take a centipede home with him. He wrote home, "I captured a centipede this afternoon, the largest one I have seen since I have been on the island. It is about six inches in length and has about fifty claws, I have it in a beer bottle – will put it in alcohol tomorrow and bring it home with me. I will try and catch a tarantula also."[140]

---

[139] *Frankfort (Ky) Roundabout*, March 8, 1899, 'Letter from Dr. Nevil M. Garrett', page 8.
[140] *The Harford (Ky) Republican*, March 24, 1899, 'Matanzas, Cuba', letter from Private A.L. Hudson;

Lt. South continued,

> *"Four big tarantulas were killed in my company's tents last night, and the little lizards sleep with us now without any case of uneasiness. At first I used to get up and shake my blankets, but now I play with them, as they are considered pets for us, and keep the flies and small insects away and are considered our best friends."*[141]

Other strange wildlife to the Kentuckians were crocodiles, a variety of native snakes and scorpions. The most devastating were mosquitoes which carried Yellow Fever, Malaria and Dengue Fever.

Other debilitating illnesses caused by changing diets, native water and life in the tropics included diarrhea, dysentery and heat stroke. Even scratches can fester quickly in the tropics and, if not treated quickly, can develop into infections. At the time of the Third Kentucky's visit to Cuba, any of these afflictions could have turned deadly.

---

[141] **Ibid, Lt. South Letter.**

CHAPTER 6

BATTALION POSTS

The regiment was divided into three battalions with the First Battalion being sent to the community of La Union de Reyes. The town was about 20 miles due south of Matanzas city and was serviced by a short line railroad. The main rail line ran from Matanzas city to Santa Clara to Havana city.

The second battalion went to Cardenas under the supervision of Colonel Smith. The battalion was to be moved by rail from Matanzas. Colonel Smith took action to order the railcars available for 6:30 p.m. on the day of movement. Three hours later the cars were still not there and the infuriated Colonel Smith went to see the local railroad superintendent -- a Spaniard -- to vent his frustrations. While Colonel Smith talked the railroad superintendent acted disinterested, continued doing his paperwork and ignored the Colonel's questions on the status of the cars. Colonel Smith "roared" and asked if the Superintendent had not heard the questions.

The Superintendent answered, "Yes".

"Then why in [expletive] blazes didn't your answer?" the Colonel asked.

...cause I am superintendent, and I am accustomed to having men remove their hats in my office," was the haughty response.

"I don't give a hang what you are," the Colonel said. "I am a sovereign in my country and you get out of that chair pretty quick and attend to those cars, or I'll telegraph Gen. Brooke about you."

The Spanish superintendent, realizing his job was at stake, took care of the issue[142].

On January 30, Carl E. Woolfolk of Company A described the movement and camp activities in a letter home to an old friend, John W. Twyman of Earlington, Kentucky. Twyman shared it with the local press. Woolfolk wrote,

> *"Our regiment has been divided, each battalion going to a different place. Union is a small place of 3,000 or 4,000 inhabitants, and is about twenty miles from Matanzas [city]. We came here on the train, making the run in two hours and fifteen minutes. I visited the principal fortifications around Matanzas and it is a strange thing to me how the Spanish expected to put up a fight against the American Navy. I don't think they had a modern breech-loading cannon in the city. All I saw were old-timers, none of which were made since 1860.*
>
> *"This is beautiful country, but the greater portion of it is overgrown with weeds, and on every hand you can see the ruins of houses and plantations. We are camped close to where a large sugar mill was destroyed about two years ago. We will have a nice camp when we get fixed up, but it will take some time to get everything in shape. We have hospital tents about fourteen feet square instead of the small tents and each man has a cot to sleep*

---

[142] **An *Atlanta Constitution* article reprinted in *The Columbus (Neb) Journal*, April 19, 1899. 'The Colonel Was Game', page 4.**

on. I believe we are going to have a much better time over here than we have had since we have been out.

"It is about as warm here now as it is in May at home. The nights are pleasant but it is as hot as summer in the middle of the day. There are lots of cocoanut trees scattered around over this part of the country, but I don't think the nuts are quite ripe. There are a good many banana trees close to where we are camped, but they, too, are unripe.

"We are quite busy getting our camp in shape, and I have hardly had time to write, so will close for this time. Kindly remember me to all enquiring friends. Tell them I am well and having a pretty good time. I expect Buck has gotten home by this time. He received a discharge in a day or two after we landed. He will tell you all about our trip."[143]

While the identity of 'Buck' is not determined, at least one man received a humanitarian discharge while in Cuba. James R. Cansler, Company A, was released from duty as a result of the distressed circumstances of his mother and sister. He had been their primary support and they were suffering as a result of his absence. A local Congressman took action to have him immediately discharged. Honorably discharged before him were James M. and Weber Breathitt.[144]

On February 5 Private August Szymanski another member of

---

[143] *The (Earlington, Ky) Bee*, February 9, 1899, 'Carl Woolfolk Writes: His First Letter from Cuban Soil—Some First Impressions', page 3.
[144] *Hopkinsville Kentuckian*, Feb. 7, 1898, 'Honorable Discharge', page 4; *Hopkinsville Kentuckian*, Feb. 21, 1899, 'Another Discharge', page 8; Several other men were discharged for a variety of reasons prior to the unit deploying to Cuba. This included Privates John Madden and W.B. Clark of Owensboro and Private W.P. Gentry of Hopkinsville. See *Hopkinsville Kentuckian*, January 13, 1899. Page 4, 'More Kentuckians Discharged'

Third Kentucky wrote his mother of camp life at Matanzas.

"We are camped on the side of the fort yet, but will move upon a hill side in a few days. The town where we were to move is in no condition for the American soldiers. There is small-pox and yellow fever there. They say we are to stay here awhile and then we are to go to Colon.

"The first battalion of the Third Kentucky is at Cardenas, the second battalion is at Union, and our battalion here at Matanzas. The population of this town is eighty-eight thousand. There are four regiments here besides our battalion. The place where we were to go has four thousand inhabitants, and there have been no soldiers there.

"There is talk that we are coming back to the United States and be mustered out in three weeks. The weather is fine here.

"I took a walk over the hills a few days ago and came across a garden. It was worth going miles to see. All kinds of vegetables were growing and everything green. The Cubans say it is this way all the year round. I went to an orange grove and got some oranges that were not quite ripe and made some lemonade out of them and it was very good. I went in the Matanzas bay and got some of the prettiest shells you ever saw. Some of them are the size of an egg and some are smaller. They are beautiful. If I live and get back home I am going to bring some to the children.

"Every soldier has a cot to himself and there are six to a tent, they are very large tents and have floors. The reason we have this is because it will keep the fever away and keep the insects from getting on the cots. The insects are very dangerous. The worst one is the tarantula. Sometimes they are with a bunch of bananas; and there are scorpion, snakes and centipedes. They are all pretty bad.

"I go to town every time I can get a pass. I like to go to see what I can see. A Cuban took us through the prison here, and it was a fine one. Everything was as clean as a pin and it was painted nicely. The flowers inside were in bloom and everything looked like spring time.

"They had a good many prisoners. It is a better prison than the one at Frankfort.

"There are lots of places here for amusement and pleasure. I have no stamps but will get some pay-day. I signed the pay-roll last Thursday. We will get paid as soon as a paymaster gets here.

"I have not seen a sign of a post office. When we mail a letter we give it to one of the men of the company and he mails it.

"Everything you buy over here is very high. Coal oil one dollar a gallon, bread ten cents a loaf, fresh beef eighty cents a pound, and every thing else is high. I have not seen any butter or eggs, but they have some very fine Jersey cattle here. The horses are smaller than the American horses and are good workers.

"I do guard duty about three times a week and fatigue duty about three times a week. I just came off of fatigue duty...

"When you answer this tell me all the news, and send me papers about two times a week. It makes a soldier as ignorant as a dog over here. We can't understand the Cubans, and can not keep up with the times in the United States because we have nothing to read."[145]

It was reported on February 6, 1899 that Private William J. Graham of the Third Kentucky died from an accidental

---

[145] *The Frankfort (KY) Roundabout*, February 18, 1899, 'Another Letter From Cuba'.

gunshot wound on January 31.¹⁴⁶ It was the same day the treaty of peace with Spain was ratified by the U.S. Senate in a vote of 57 for, 27 against and six absent. The vote passed with two more votes than were necessary.

Private A.L. Hudson of Company D wrote home on February 9 to inform the folks of his hometown of Hartford of the experiences of the troops at Matanzas, Cuba. He urged the editor to continue sending *The Hartford Republican* to his deployed address saying, "We Hartford boys miss it very much, especially over here in Cuba, where an English almanac is considered good reading."

He updated readers on Company D, then in the third battalion, which he said

> *"is all right. Captain Keown and 44 of his men are in charge of the Fort which contains the military prison. There are about 75 prisoners in there and it keeps the Captain and his men on duty most all of the time to keep everything straight. The General inspects the prison every day and everything has to be carried on in a military style or some one gets jacked up. The General seems well pleased with the way Captain Keown conducts his business, in fact he compliments him most every time he comes out to camp."*

Hudson described the camp as "just in the edge of the city limits. It is a pretty rough camp but we are being as comfortably fixed as could be asked. Every man has been issued a cot and have good tents with floors in them."

He described the disposition of troops noting,

---

[146] *The (Maysville, KY) Evening Bulletin,* **February 6, 1899, 'Deaths in Havana Camps';** *Omaha Daily Bee,* **February 5, 1899, 'Death Report from Cuba'**

> *"There is only one battalion of our regiment here. The first battalion, with Major Saffron in command, is stationed at Union, Cuba. The four companies that constitute the first are Co. A, of Madisonville; Co. G, of Glasgow; Co. K, of Paducah, and Co. C, of Bardstown. The second battalion, with Col. Smith in command, is stationed at Cardenas, with Co. M, of Winchester; Co. B, of Bowling Green; Co. F, of Owensboro, and Co. L, of Lexington. The third battalion is commanded by Lt. Col. Henry, with Co. J, of Morgantown; Co. E, of Hopkinsville; Co. D of Hartford, and Co. H, of Henderson. The boys seem to be very well satisfied. Of course, there are some who are not, but had just as well be, for Uncle Sam has got them where the wool won't slip."*

Hudson described Matanzas saying,

> *"Matanzas, under the governorship of Gen. Wilson, is or will be from all indications, one of the nicest cities on the island when the Spanish filth is all cleaned up. It was one of the filthiest places on the globe, when the volunteers arrived here. The city and forts were once very fine places, but they had been neglected and let go until it will cost our government considerable money and hard labor to have them put in good shape.*

> *"The houses, with few exceptions, are built of stone. There are some very fine buildings, which must have cost a great deal of money, such as the plaza, cathedral, theatrical and numerous others buildings that I have been unable to find out what they are used for.*

> *"The streets are being cleaned every day, which will be of great benefit to the health of the people. They are bound to be more or less unhealthy, for the streets are not at the greatest over 40 feet wide with a three and one-half foot sidewalk on each side. The town is laid off in blocks as our cities. One solid wall runs the full block, partitioned off about every thirty feet, in the center of this thirty foot room is a door, on each side of the door is a*

window. The doors are heavy and the windows are protected by heavy iron bars, not only a few of them, but all of them. A house doesn't seem complete here if not finished that way. I have noticed about four or five frame houses, but they are ready to fall at any time and are of modern type. The stone buildings are built of rough stone and then plastered to a smooth finish. The farmers through the country have everything built of stone, all outbuildings, fences, water troughs and anything that we would build of lumber, they build of the same stone and they will last for generations to come.

"There are a great many intelligent people here, but the principal portion of the wealthy business men are Spaniards. The Spanish treat us with much more courtesy than the Cubans do. The Cubans are a treacherous set of people. The government is working a great many of them. They come to work with a big knife swung to them. They all carry a knife or dirk. The knives they carry are about like our corn knives and of all description.

"Well I could write all night and then not give you but a hint of the different things and people. There are some very fine looking people here – more so in the female sex – but we can't talk to them, they say, 'we no comprehendo.'

"Well, as it is 'Tapps' now and the lights must be blown out, I will close, hoping that if you deem this any news that will interest your readers you will publish it."[147]

Hudson wrote again on March 10 noting Company D;

"is getting their fair share of duty as the boys only get off one day out of every five. Is all guard duty, they stand guard 24 hours, on two and off four and the next 24 hours they are on fatigue guard

---

[147] ***The Hartford (Ky) Republican,*** **February 24, 1899, 'Soldier Letter: Our Correspondent Tells How Things Are Managed in Camp Severino, Matanzas, Cuba, also Other Good Items', page 1.**

– guarding prisoners while they are out at work, they take about fifty of them out at 7 o'clock a.m. and come in at 11 o'clock, go out again at 1 p.m. and come in at four. They get a pass every fifth day to visit the city. The duty is some lighter on the boys now as three of our company who were left in Columbus, Ga., on provost guard came to us a few days ago. It seems that when they want things properly guarded they call on Co. D., for instance when Capt. Keown was put in command of the Fort it was customary to change the fort guard every ten days by putting in a different company, but Co. D has made such an able impression on the Generals that he cannot get a change.

"Lieutenant Oscar Bishop and Corporal Ira Ragland visited the city of Havana a few days ago, and of course came back with such reports that makes others want to go there. They saw the wreck of the Maine, Morro Castle and numerous other sights --- they will tell you all about it when they get home…

"…One could not wonder at everything being built of rock here, for there is nothing here but rock. The weather is very pleasant here at present with exception of the strong wind which causes the dust to fly at times so one can scarcely see.

"Major [James C.] Bryant while out on a skiff riding in the Bay yesterday afternoon came in contact with a few pretty large waves and broke one of his skiff oars and then you should have heard him yell for someone to tow him ashore. Lieut. Payne who is assisting Capt. Keown in the fort heard his yells of distress and ran to the water edge, but by the time the Lieutenant had got there he had gotten near the fort and landed safely in the bath entrance of the fort…".[148]

The Third Battalion's Dr. Nevil M. Garrett maintained a small hospital in Matanzas. He wrote the hospital was "very

---

[148] *The Hartford (Ky) Republican*, March 24, 1899, 'Matanzas, Cuba' page 1.

nicely fixed. One defect has been the diet" of the patients. Dr. Garrett's professionalism was such he noted the Army's chief surgeon "would like to have me in the regular army...I'm like most of the boys, 'I want to go home'."[149]

He also remarked on the tropical gardens noting, "This must have been a pretty country before the war. I was around on the other side of the bay recently, and saw one or two lovely gardens, but gardens containing plants and such."[150]

Second Lieutenant Rob Malin of Company F also wrote to his hometown newspaper about the second battalion's location at Cardenas. He said, "The Kentucky boys have gotten the best of the deal in assignment to garrison duty in Cuba, and the second battalion of the Third Kentucky is stationed at Cardenas, a city of about 23,000 inhabitants said to be the cleanest city on the island." He noted some of the people spoke English and "have to a certain extent adopted American ways." He too described the houses made of stone, with tile roofs and tile floors, shuttered windows with iron grating and doors made of "heavy solid timber." Malin noted the houses had no front yards but, if a yard existed, was in the "rear of the house and is filled with flowers and evergreens...If a family have a carriage it is kept in the room next to the sitting room and the horse in a room in the rea of the house. The houses of the best people are beautifully furnished, the furniture all being mahogany."[151]

He said the exchange rate was one American dollar for a 1.20 or 1.40 in Spanish silver. The Spanish did not have a nickel but one and two cent pieces made of copper. He observed,

---

[149] *Frankfort (Ky) Roundabout,* **March 18, 1899, 'Letter from Dr. Nevil M. Garrett', page 8.**
[150] **Ibid.**
[151] *The Breckenridge News,* **March 8, 1898, 'They Sell Cheap Jags'. The Lieutenant wrote his letter on February 18, 1899.**

"There are a good many U.S. 5-cent silver pieces that were taken in by Spain, a hole punched in them and used as 2 ½ cent pieces."

He noted the prices of local goods. Armour & Co. small canvass hams sold for 35 cent a pound, eggs were five cents each, and to order one cooked at a restaurant cost twenty cents. A small chicken, cooked, cost $1.75. Malin said, "The only thing you can get cheap here is a drink. You can get a drink for two cents and after you have taken three drinks you will be drunk for three days."

Lt. South was more detailed in relaying the price of alcohol. He said Cognac brandy was two cents a glass; a bottle of fine wine was three cents a glass and a glass of lemonade was a penny.

Malin also described local transport of fodder. He wrote;

Cuban Transporting Fodder *(Taylor Papers)*

"The roads are very bad. Grass for the stock is brought in from the country on the backs of ponies. You will see what you think is a shock of hay coming down the street, but on examination you

will find a pony under it and tied to that pony's tail you will find a rope and at the end of the rope, or halter, another pony with another stack of hay on its back. I have seen from three to four tied together this way and to the last pony's tail would be tied a dog."

He also described local burial practices noting,

"I visited the cemetery a few days ago and found that the wealthy people have some very find vaults in which to put their dead. The poor people are rented a place for a grave at so much a month and when the relatives or friends of the dead fail to pay the body is taken up and either burned or thrown into a large pit walled with stones and fitted for the purpose. I looked into it and saw skeletons from which all the flesh had not decayed."

Malin also took the time to describe the fairer sex. He said,

"The young ladies use a good deal of powder and never wear a hat even when they go out in the hot sun. They never go on the street without a chaperon even in the day time. When you call on a girl you see her in the sitting room with the rest of the family. Wonder how that would suit some of the boys in the States? The young people are never left to themselves until after they are engaged. A young lady never goes out anywhere after she is engaged until she is married. Some of the girls in the wealthy families were sent to the United States during the last two years of the war and learned to speak some English and we some times get a head of the old folks that way. There are some of the prettiest girls here I ever saw, but for all that old Kentucky is good enough for me."[152]

Lt South also said he could not

"do justice to the beauty of the Cuban muchachas, or girls. They

---

[152] Ibid, 'They Sell Cheap Jags', letter from 2nd Lt. Rob Malin, Co. F, in Cardenas, Cuba, February 18, 1899.

are without question, the most beautiful women I ever saw, all of them are brunettes or the most pronounced type...all dress elegantly in what we would call a summer dress and wear white cloth shoes and affect much fine lace, especially about the head. Many wear their hair loose (and often it touches the ground) and no hats or head gear at all; their hair is as black as a crow's wing, so black that it glitters."

He also noted that he was speaking of "the richer class".[153]

The first battalion at Camp Tyrman in La Union also had a correspondent to a local newspaper, specifically the *Hartford Herald*. A.P. Minton of Company A wrote on February 24,

"While the people of old Kentucky are shivering around the hearthstone, the boys of the Third Kentucky are sweating in the heat of Cuba. Though we are in the tropics the ragged end of the cold wave that swept over the States reached us. Last week the thermometer dropped from 85 degrees to about 60. The thermometer reaches 95 sometimes during the day now, though the nights are always cool.

"This battalion (the first) is in one of the finest sections of Cuba. We are in a broad valley that shows that it was in a high state of cultivation before the war laid it in waste. But everywhere the ravages of war are apparent. Sugar mills were destroyed and dwellings made desolate...Near our camp are the ruins of Santa Ross, said to have been one of the finest sugar mills in Cuba...The park and flower gardens though in ruins and neglected, show that a vast amount of money was spent in beautifying and in making the home a paradise.

"There are four sugar mills in sight of our camp. They are the only things here that are modern in appearance. They are all fitted up with modern machinery and the operators seem to have

---

[153] **Ibid, Lt. South letter.**

learned the principal of utilizing all waste matter. The cane is run through several sets of rollers until it is perfectly dry, then carried through a chute to engines and furnaces, where it is used as fuel, being almost the only fuel used.

"There is but little fruit raised in this section, as the land can be easily cultivated on account of being level, and level land is not so common in Cuba as it is in America. Sugar cane is most profitable. There is but little tobacco raised around here, but they have it in all stages of growth, setting out and cutting at the same time.

"The native Cubans as a class are not the most cleanly and refined people on earth. I have seen dogs, cats, goats, chickens, turkeys, horses, cows, babies and about fifteen children, all living under the same roof and not a very big roof either. I do not wonder at them having yellow fever, small-pox and kindred diseases."[154]

The *Hickman Courier* also had a correspondent, Jim Robertson of Company K, first battalion, who wrote home about the same time from La Union. He also shared extensive observations of Cuba and Cubans. Said Robertson,

"While alone tonight with nothing to bother me but a parrot, dog and a few mosquitoes, my thoughts have wandered back to the many friends far away in old Kentucky...It is a sight never to be forgotten, the poor and destitute standing around the mess room begging us for the scraps or searching the slop cans for something to eat...While at Matanzas, we camped near [an] old Fort [Severino] a grand old structure, placed there some 300 years ago. It has a good command of the Bay, and the six inch brass guns, set upon the ramparts would have been no match to our 13 inch

---

[154] *The Hartford (Ky) Herald*, **March 8, 1899, 'Letter from Cuba', February 24, 1899, Letter from A.P. Minton, Company A, Third Kentucky Infantry, USV.**

guns 4 or 5 miles at sea. This old Fort has a history that I will not undertake to write now.

"The cruelty and barbarism perpetrated upon the poor unfortunate Cubans within these walls is too awful to mention. I stood upon the stone which the Spaniards used for a chopping and was told by a Cuban that 300 Cubans' heads were chopped off on that stone in one night.

"I spent four months in Porto Rico last summer but find Cuba is far ahead of her, for in Porto Rico there is nothing but mountains, the people live on fruits and are a thousand years behind the times. Here it is different, the lay of the land has palms, oranges and banana groves. The flowers and vegetable gardens, the lovely valleys and babbling brooks make one feel that he has found a Paradise on earth.

"All that I can see that is needed here is a people of our kind, then this could be made a great country. In La Union I find the town full of interesting buildings, many of them bearing signs of grandeur and elegance of a more prosperous day. The town has no doubt been one of wealth and culture, but the war has left its imprints, and everything points to neglect and poverty.

"Many of the residences or palaces they are called here, have marble floors, marble base boards, walls elegantly frescoed and courts in the rear where tropical plants grow and bloom in great [quantities].

"The white Cuban girls are very intelligent people and generally good-looking, and some are real pretty, but all of them are just as vain as the Kentucky girls, judging from the lavish hand with which they apply powder to their countenance, which looks as if they had applied with a white wash brush. They come out to the camp every Monday eve which is Sunday in this country all [decked] out in their best and they don't look bad either, but the children are dressed very scantily, and a yard of calico would

make a dozen dresses [for the children].

"*I have seen the rosy side of life among the natives who seem to live in ease and luxury. They rise at 7 o'clock and taking breakfast at 9 o'clock, then they sleep until 2 when they have lunch and dress for the afternoon ride around the city until 6:30, when they have dinner; and on the other hand I have seen the bitter life, led by the unfortunate ones, many of whom are half starved. I saw women and children sleeping in halls, doorways, alleys and on the sidewalks, just any old place that will afford temporary lodging.*

"*I was told by a native who speaks English very plainly that a young man in courting a young lady was not allowed in the parlor under a years' time but has to stand on the side walk and talk to her through the iron bars in front of the windows, and then with the old lady near by. After he has carried it on in that way for a year he is allowed to talk to her alone in the parlor for six months. Then he must marry or quit and make room for another one.*

"*The feature of this place that strikes me more favorable is that one of our dollars is worth a dollar and forty cents of their money. A fellow could come over here with a thousand dollars and get it changed up and be a millionaire, but he would have to get a wagon to carry the change off, because in changing a dollar, one gets a hatful in return, some of their largest pieces being worth only 2 cents.*

"*If there is anyone on earth the Cubans hate it is the Spaniards, but the Spaniards are all very nice to us, but of course it is policy for them to be so.*"[155]

---

[155] *The Hickman (Ky) Courier,* **March 10, 1899, 'Hickman Boy In Cuba: the Country, Social Conditions, &c', Letter from Jim Robertson, Co. K, Third Kentucky, La Union, Cuba**

On February 22nd General Maximo Gomez y Baez, Cuba's military commander during their three year war of independence, arrived in Matanzas city by rail where he was met and feted by Major General James H. Wilson, the U.S. military governor of the province. Also in the reception group were General Joseph P. Sanger, U.S. military governor of the district and city of Matanzas and Matanzas Cuban Forces commander General Pedro E. Betancourt. General Gomez was escorted from the railway station to the Governor's palace under the escort of the Eighth Massachusetts Volunteer Infantry and the Second U.S. Cavalry. He was honored with a reception that night and a banquet the next day.

General Gomez visited the Spanish Club where "a committee of Spaniards waited upon him to say that they desired to express their acceptance of his policy of amalgamation". Gomez was gracious in reply stating "the war should be forgotten and all the enmities of the past buried." This followed with an inspection of the American military encampment. Gomez was reportedly met and escorted at Cardenas by Third Kentucky Colonel Thomas J. Smith and the Second Battalion in what was billed as "the beginning of the Cuban triumphal procession and entry into the city of Havana, a historic episode in Cuban affairs and hence in the affairs of this country." The Third Kentucky likely were an impressive sight as Army Inspector General Brigadier General J.C. Breckinridge praised the regiment's professionalism noting "if the Third kept to its present standard it would be mustered out with the distinction of being one of the very best regiments in the volunteer army". [156]

---

[156] *The Bourbon (Paris, Ky) News*, **February 24, 1899, 'Gen. Gomez at Matanzas: He Dined with the Spanish Club, Visited the American Camp and Attended a Ball', 2**

Gomez was honored with a formal ball that evening hosted by General Wilson. Among the special guests for the ball was General Adna Chaffee, Chief of Staff to U.S. Military Governor in Cuba, General Leonard Wood. Also invited were "all the prominent people of the city, Cubans and Spaniards, without distinction, were present."[157]

In early February General Wilson reported there was no disorder "of any kind" in Matanzas Province. There were however renegade soldiers still in the countryside. One newspaper reported,

> *"Brigandage is reported from Matanzas province, but it met with heroic treatment. A party of seven bandits, alleged to be former Spanish guerillas, led by a negro guide named Vidal, began the depredations. A squad of Cuban soldiers under Major Arguellas pursued and overtook the band near the hamlet of Cartagena, where two of the bandits were killed and two wounded. The Cubans lost one killed and two wounded. The pursuit continued."*[158]

On March 2nd the second battalion was relocated to Matanzas. Colonel Smith was reported sick and a soldier named Turner was suffering from dysentery and sent to the Department Hospital. The regimental Provost Guards that had been left in Columbus arrived at Matanzas on March 4th and rumors were already circulating that the regiment would be demobilized and returned home.[159]

---

[157] Ibid; *Daily Public Ledger* (Maysville, Ky), February 22, 1899, 'Gen. Gomez at Matanzas', page 3'; *The (Maysville, Ky) Evening Bulletin*, March 2, 1899, 'Third Kentucky', page 2.
[158] *The Scranton Tribune*, February 7, 1899, p.4; *The (Maysville, Ky) Evening Bulletin*, February 24, 1899, 'Routing Cuban Brigands', page 1.
[159] *Frankfort (Ky) Roundabout*, March 18, 1899, 'Letter from Dr. Nevil M. Garrett', page 8; see also The Harford Republican, March 24, 1899, 'Matanzas, Cuba', letter from Private A.L. Hudson; *The*

In late March however there were reports of 'outlaws' raiding plantations in Matanzas and neighboring provinces to steal horses and cattle. The Cuban troops in the district were charged with chasing the bandits. No U.S. troops were used.[160]

Eldred Davis, Company A, wrote a letter to the editor of the Earlington, *Kentucky Bee* on March 4 also telling of the First Battalion's outpost at La Union. He said La Union,

> *"has about 3,000 inhabitants, but about 2,500 are worthless and indolent. They could, if they so desired, make La Union the garden spot of the Province. I would like to see a man like that benevolent benefactor of Earlington, come among these lazy people with his Yankee grit and determination. I venture the assertion that within a short time, you would see a beautiful little town spring up from amid the heaps of ruin and filth. Its location is healthful, as it is situated on high ground, about twenty-five miles from Matanzas, and about five miles east of Alfonza XII.*
>
> *"Our camp is surrounded by stately palm trees, making it very picturesque. There are many sugar plants in the immediate vicinity, from which we obtain an unlimited supply of crude sugar and Cuban syrup, gladly given us by the owners of the various plants.*
>
> *"Cigars, etc., are very cheap, as the natives consider smoking almost as essential as eating. Everybody smokes, from the small child to the grandmother. Everything raised or made on the Island is very cheap, but all the imported stuff is very high, especially writing paper. (I obtained this by violating the seventh commandment.[161])*

Hartford (Ky) Republican, **March 24, 1899, 'Matanzas, Cuba', March 10 letter from A.L. Hudson.**
[160] *Houston Daily Post*, **April 6, 1899, 'Chasing Marauders', page 4.**
[161] **"Thou Shalt Not Steal".**

"We have plenty of fruit but it is very unripe, although the boys eat it; consequently we have a great deal of sickness but very little in Company A.

"The days are very warm but night very cool, and one could sleep well, were it not for the insects and the reptiles. They take a delight in playing hide and seek on our blankets.

"We are living well now for army life, getting plenty of pork and beans, because we now have a commissary officer who looks after his men, and, to use an army term, "He is a grafter." Therefore Lieut. Paul P. Price is a favorite with both men and officers.

"I would like to visit Cuba again but not in blue clothes. I would like to return on upper deck and take turn about with the captain of the ship, looking through those big glasses. We hope to come home before the rainy season sets in, and when we do our parents can lay in a new supply of groceries. True to the old saying, we are coming home to die, but we wish to die that sublime death of overtaxing our digestive organs.

"We await impatiently the arrival of The Bee each week. It seems like an old friend. Well, I fancy I have taken up too much of your valuable space, so with kindest regards to all friends, and wishing The Bee a successful voyage each week,"[162]

The men had the presence of a YMCA. Third Kentucky Chaplain Frank M. Thomas wrote from his post in Cardenas, "It is the unanimous exclamation of the Kentucky troops that the Y.M.C.A. is the best thing in the army. When the regiment was separated into battalions each battalion begged for the Y.M.C.A. tent."[163]

---

[162] *The (Earlington, Ky) Bee,* **March 16, 1899, "Third Kentucky: Letter from Eldred Davis with Interesting Information', page 2**
[163] *The (Maysville) Evening Bulletin,* **March 30, 1899**

Not all activity occurred at the YMCA however. Men could get into town for some down time that included gambling houses and bars. It was during one such foray that Vanceburg's Captain Allen W. Brewer of Company M made a unique find in Cardenas. It was reported he

> *"discovered possibly the oldest bottle of whisky in the world. It was made at Frankfort [Kentucky] in 1838 by the elder Pepper, and had been in stock at a Cardenas café for forty years."*[164]

In March a correspondent in Matanzas wrote a report to the *Bowling Green Times* there was speculation that Lt. Col. Jouett Henry wound throw his hat in the ring for the Democratic nomination for Lieutenant Governor when he was demobilized. His competence was such that he had been selected in late January by Major General Wilson to command the city of Colon for a period. The reporter wrote,

> *"he does not care to discuss politics while he is a soldier, but those who are his closest friends are talking for him, and in their enthusiasm declare that the buzz of the political bee is almost audible in his bonnet."*

The reporter described Henry as an "anti-imperialist free silver William J. Bryan Democrat of the most pronounced type. He is universally popular in the regiment."[165]

He also made note of the First Battalion's encampment at La Union writing,

> *"Surgeon Major Bell returned yesterday from inspecting the First battalion at La Union. He reports the health of the men at that place good and the sanitary conditions of the camp perfect. Major*

---

[164] *The (Maysville) Daily Public Ledger*, February 27, 1899, page 4.
[165] *Hopkinsville Kentuckian*, March 21, 1899, 'Col. Henry's Ambition: Will Likely Be A Candidate for Lieut. Governor', page 4; *The Bee*, February 2, 1899, 'Lieut. Col. Henry'

*Safferans and his men hope to **remain** at La Union until the transport comes to carry the regiment home. La Union is in the very heart of the great sugar producing region of Matanzas province and the wealthy planters of that vicinity are said to be making the stay of the soldiers **more** pleasant than they expected."*[166]

It was publicly announced on March 20 that the Third Kentucky would be mustered out of service in Savannah in the middle of April. This was later changed and Gov. Bradley was notified on April 21 that the Third Kentucky would be formally mustered out on May 16. The men were to be paid at the "war rate" of $14.60 a month rather than the peacetime rate of $13 a month.[167] Further, by mustering out in Savannah the men were entitled to travel pay of $32.80 of which $15 would be used to get them home leaving each man a small profit of $17.80. They would lose this if mustered out in Lexington or closer to home and would still have to pay their own way home.[168]

Colonel Smith took an advance party to Savannah to make arrangements to receive and support the regiment's demobilization.[169]

---

[166] Ibid.
[167] *The Bee*, March 23, 1899, 'Third Kentucky'; *The Hickman (Ky) Courier*, March 1899, page 4; *The Hartford (Ky) Herald*, April 26, 1899, 'The Latest News', page 3; *The (Lancaster, Ky) Central Record*, April 27, 1899, *Hopkinsville Kentuckian*, April 25, 1899, 'Mustering Out Date', page 2; 'On May 16: Soldier Boys Will Soon Come Marching Home', page 8; The Bee, April 27, 1899, 'The Day Is Set: Third Kentucky to Be Mustered Out May 16', page 2.
[168] *The (Earlington, Ky) Bee*, March 30, 1899, 'Regiment Prefers Savannah', page 3. Travel pay included mileage home and one extra day of extra pay for every 20 miles. See *The Richmond (Ky) Climax*, March 15, 1899, 'The Third Kentucky Mustered Out', page3.
[169] *Hopkinsville Kentuckian*, April 25, 1899, 'Third Kentucky In Camp' page 7

CHAPTER 7

DEMOBILIZATION AND HOME

The return trip by ship was uncomfortable as the seas were rough. It was reported, "A greater part of the command was dreadfully sick."[170]

The men arrived at the quarantine station a Daufuskie Island outside of Savannah on April 14th for five days of delousing and medical inspection. According to a news report

> *"At the quarantine station the men were called on to surrender for the first time since they departed from the States. All their personal effects and the regimental baggage had to be given to the Government surgeons, who threw everything into large chests and then injected fumes of formaldehyde gas. To some of the men this was not altogether pleasing, but it was no more than their predecessors had experienced, some of whom were heavy losers…After the detention period the regiment will be brought to*

---

[170] *Frankfort (Ky) Roundabout*, April 15, 1899, 'Sea Sick', page 3.

the city on lighters, and will be camped south of town pending the muster out, which it is expected will be within the next three weeks."[171]

Four men were still on duty in Cuba. Among them was Captain Noel Gaines who was in charge of the relief work in Havana. Gaines had been on detached service to the staff of First Army Corps Commander Major General William Ludlow, Military Governor Commanding the Department of Havana since soon after his arrival in late December 1898. He went to Cuba earlier than the unit because Ludlow, impressed by Gaines' work in Columbus, Georgia, requested his staff appointment from the Secretary of War which was granted.

In this capacity Gaines was responsible for overseeing the distribution of Army rations to the poor of Havana. In what one may view as an early version of the post-World War II Marshall Plan, it was reported the "supplies have done so much to alleviate local suffering and saved hundreds of lives."

Gaines was credited with feeding up to 20,000 of Havana's poor, issuing over one million rations. His work gained the attention of his superiors leading to a recommendation for promotion to Major in April. Gaines' efforts were such that the leaders of 30 benevolent societies operating in that city sent a petition to U.S. leadership asking that Gaines be retained on active service. A similar petition had been sent by Cuban military officers and it was reported that General Ludlow would request Captain Gaines be appointed to his staff after formally being mustered out.[172]

---

[171] *Hopkinsville Kentuckian*, April 14, 1899, 'Third KY. Arrives'.
[172] *The Omaha Daily Bee*, May 4, 1899, 'Better Health in Havana', page 1; *The Frankfort Roundabout*, April 15, 1899, a front page reprint of an article in the *Havana (Cuba) Daily Advertiser*, March 27, 1899.

Another officer reportedly remaining behind was Lieutenant Robert C. Payne of Company E. Since his arrival in Cuba Payne had been on detached duty serving as the commander of the old Spanish Fort San Severino, then serving as the home to 86 civil prisoners. Payne made note that his objective was to remain in the Army in some capacity and to go to Manila whenever the Third Kentucky was mustered out.[173]

The regiment left quarantine on April 18 and arrived at the Savannah wharves where they were put into regimental formation. At about 3 p.m., with Colonel Smith at the head of the regiment, they set off to the Savannah encampment – known as Camp *Onward* -- marching through the middle of the city. According to a report, "The scene was picturesque and inspiring as the regiment tramped over the principal streets, the band playing and the men cheering. Citizens caught the spirit of the movement and also cheered."[174]

On May 6 while waiting in Savannah, a War Department order put a damper on officer morale as they were being demobilized. The War Department wanted to ensure each officer's account was audited in Washington to prevent overpayment and ensure recoupment of debt for clothing and ordinance accounts as well as account for Army property which the officers signed for when assuming command.

Army authorities ruled "that volunteer officers of the army, who are responsible for public property, shall be paid only mileage and travel allowances hereafter until they have accounted for all public property for which they are responsible, so the officers of the 3rd Kentucky will not get their four months' pay on being mustered out."

---

[173] *Hopkinsville Kentuckian*, **April 11, 1899, 'Bob Payne: Commander of A Spanish Fort and Not Coming Home', page 5**
[174] **Ibid,** *Hopkinsville Kentuckian*, **'Third Kentucky in Camp';**

Holding back one month's pay had been normal procedure but never had anyone been denied their entire pay. The officers had not been paid since February. Further, all officers and men who saw foreign service were entitled to two months extra pay when discharged. It was anticipated this new order was going to delay pay for several more months and morale plummeted. An additional detail was that, as a result of the date of the order, the Army paymaster determined it only impacted the Third Kentucky and none of the other units in Savannah would be impacted. The Third Kentucky felt they were being unfairly discriminated against and they objected to this discrimination through the chain of command.[175]

Tragedy struck the Third Kentucky while in Savannah. Private James Arnold of Company I was handling a weapon when it accidentally discharged killing Private Herman Hunt and seriously wounded Private Edward Allen. According to reports,

> "The shooting was done with an old Remington rifle that had been brought from Cuba as a relic. Arnold was sitting in his tent, inserting a cartridge in the gun, when it was discharged. The bullet went through the wall of the tent and passed through the body of Private Hunt and broke the arm of Allen. Arnold is under arrest, pending examination, but it is not believed the shooting was anything but accidental."[176]

Another report indicated Hunt was shot in the abdomen and lingered for about eight hours before dying. Hunt was described as a "good and faithful soldier" who was "loved by all and to know him was to admire his great morals, and such

---

[175] *Hopkinsville Kentuckian*, May 19, 1899, 'Kentuckians Hard Hit: Four Month's Pay of Officers of the Third Will Be Held Up'; *The (Stanford, Ky) Semi-Weekly Interior Journal*, May 9, 1899, 'Soldier and Sailor Intelligence', page 4.
[176] Ibid, *Semi-Weekly*, May 9, 1899; *Accomac (Va) Peninsula Enterprise*, May 13, 1899, page 4.

a light as God would use to woo the world to grace...".[177] He was survived by his wife.

The same report indicated the bullet entered Allen's body "just above the elbow, crushing the bone and severing the main artery, causing a great loss of blood before the surgeons, who were quickly summoned, could arrive and stop the flow."

Going Home
On May 16, 1899, the Third Kentucky Volunteer Infantry was formally mustered out of Federal service in Savannah, Georgia with one year and nine days service. They began the return trip to their old Kentucky homes. Colonel Smith worked to ensure everyone was paid. One report said

> *"three paymasters had the job of paying off. They commenced their work about 8 o'clock a.m., and by 12 o'clock, m., every man had been paid off and discharged. They were as fine a body of men as ever shouldered a gun, and made a record, while in the service, of which their State may well be proud."*[178]

The trips home were not uneventful. One news report called members of the unit "Kentucky Hoodlums" noting,

> *"A number of mustered out Third Kentucky soldiers who passed through [Chattanooga] en route home [on May 18] created [a] good deal of terror and wrought more or less damage along the line to Lexington by firing promiscuously from the car windows. When their special train left the Central depot the men who were drinking heavily opened fire on the passenger and freight trains*

---

[177] *The Hartford Republican*, May 12, 1899, p3, 'A Sad Accident in Co. I of the Third Kentucky'.
[178] *The Frankfort (Ky) Roundabout*, May 20, 1899, 'Third Kentucky Returns Home', page 3; Hopkinsville Kentuckian, May 16, 1899, 'Coming Home: Soldiers Boys From Cuba Expected This Week', page 6.

that answered for a target. At the Chattanooga driving park they fired upon a number of blooded horses, killing it is said two of them and wounding others. Many of the stations along the line were perforated with lead and a message was sent up the road for all agents to be on the lookout to avoid being shot."[179]

Colonel Smith heard of the report and contacted Major James C. Bryant of the 3rd Battalion as it was allegedly occurred on the 3rd Battalion's train home. Major Bryant disputed the charges and made the following statement:

"I have just received a letter from Col. Smith telling me that a soldier returning home on the section of the train with me fired off his pistol while passing out of Chattanooga, and that the shot killed a horse. I have made a thorough investigation and find that the statement is untrue.

"They never fired a gun while passing through any town or city, and their treatment of me was polite and respectful at all times. To show you that this statement is not exaggerated, while the boys have been badly treated by the officials of the Georgia & Alabama railroad, who gave us the meanest of accommodations, I will but refer to the condition of the cars bringing us here. The cars were dirty and worn out. The officials wanted us to go by the Louisville & Nashville, 200 or 300 miles out of our way, and because they were refused we were crowded into three musty coaches. The men protested against such treatment, and, it is true made a great many threats. These threats had their effect too, for more cars were finally given us."[180]

The 3rd Battalion arrived home on May 17. All were described

---

[179] Reprint of *Chattanooga Star* article in *The Topeka (KS) State Journal,* May 18, 1899, 'Kentucky Hoodlums: Shoot from Car Windows at Everything in Sight', page 5.
[180] *Hickman (Ky) Courier,* May 26, 1899, 'Not A Shot Was Fired'.

in "good health" and "glad to get back home".[181]

About 30 troops from Hopkinsville returned home on May 19 on one of the first trains. While the reunions were happy and the men treated to a dinner and dance at the armory, the return trip was not without tragedy. Private Mike Pritchett, Company A, of Madisonville "fell under a train at a station in Georgia and had one leg so badly mangled that it had to be cut off. Dr. Bell left him in charge of local surgeons." Additionally Gano Bullard "broke a finger playing ball" in Savannah and "was having trouble with his hand that may make amputation necessary." The finger would not heal and caused Bullard so much trouble that it was amputated in June.[182]

Hopkins County's Company A were extended

> *"a hearty welcome by the people...The welcome...could not have been more cordial...Madisonville was decorated and in holiday attire, and for the first time the Mecca of many visitors who had friends among the boys in blue or wanted to help receive them. Speeches were made, bands played and everything belonged to the boys. The Bee joins in the welcome. Welcome home to peaceful pursuits, to long, sober and prosperous lives, to every good thing that life affords, and may there be never another occasion for the call to war to stir the blood of patriotic young and old in America. The American Volunteer has taught foreign nations a lesson they will not soon forget, but one the American Volunteer ever holds himself in readiness to repeat."*[183]

---

[181] Ibid, 'Kentucky Soldiers Arrive Home'; *The Bee*, April 27, 1899, 'The Day Is Set: Third Kentucky to Be Mustered Out May 16', page 2.

[182] *Hopkinsville Kentuckian*, Friday, May 19, 1899, 'Home Once More', page 1; *Hopkinsville Kentuckian*, June 15, 1899, 'Took Off Finger', page 8.

[183] *The (Earlington, Ky) Bee*, May 25, 1899, 'Happy Welcome Home', page 1.

Paducah City Council also appropriated $200 to entertain Company L in local celebrations when they returned home.[184] Captain Gaines' Company returned to Frankfort without any advance warning "so there was no chance to give them a reception" according to local press reports. The report said, "The boys brought a number of curiosities home with them, and, are giving pleasure to their friends by exhibiting them. One or two Cubans were also brought along as their mascots."[185]

At least one officer and several enlisted me brought home Cuban orphans. As many of these young men were single and on the road, their charges were often given to family members to raise.

Reportedly First Lieutenant Samuel F. South[186] of Company H, the Henderson company,

> *"found a little Cuban boy, whose father and mother had been murdered by the Spanish. Taking pity upon the little waif, he cared for him during the time the regiment was in Cuba, and, when the time came to return to the United States, the little fellow would not consent to be left, and Lieut. South brought him with him to this city. The little chap is a bright and sprightly little one, and is a great pet with everybody who has seen him."*[187]

The "little waif" was christened 'Henry South' and was listed in the 1900 Federal Census as the adopted son of John H. South and Susan South of Switzer, Franklin County,

---

[184] *The (Earlington, Ky) Bee*, May 11, 1899, page 1
[185] *The Frankfort (Ky) Roundabout*, May 27, 1899, 'Frankfort Boys Get Home', page 4.
[186] Samuel Fogg South was born October 20, 1868 in Franklin County, Kentucky and died at the age of 75 on July 17, 1944 in the Veterans Administration hospital in Lexington, Fayette County, Kentucky.
[187] Ibid, 'Brings A Cuban Boy Home With Him', page 4.

Kentucky. John was the older brother of Samuel South.[188]

The Third Kentucky's Sidney Boles also apparently brought an orphan home. The 1900 census shows Joaquin Machado, age 10, as an adopted son in the household of Sam and Mary Boles, ages 75 and 71, respectively. Also in the household are a daughter, Jamie L., 41 and son Sid, 35. Sidney was a Corporal and later Quartermaster Sergeant for Company G, 3rd Kentucky.[189]

In Owensboro in the Walp household in 1900 is found Andrew Lopez, age 13, born in Cuba and listed as the 'adopted son' of Charles and Cotties H. Walp, ages 46 and 41, respectively. Also in the household are Mr. Walp's mother and the couple's four natural children, Rufus E., 22; Mintie B., 20; Charley H, 17 and Ema C., 13. Rufus Walp had been a Corporal in Company F, Third Kentucky in Cuba.[190]

Paul D. and Mildred Henderson also had an 'adopted son' from Cuba in their Rocky Hill home in Barren County, Kentucky. His name was Ralph Hachow or Mochow and he was 12 years of age. There's no record of Mr. Henderson serving however there are three Henderson men who served in the Third Kentucky.[191] The Robert J. Moore household also had two daughters, age 2, and an adopted son from Cuba identified as Joe Moore, age 15. There is no record of Robert J. Moore serving in the Third Kentucky.[192] The Ben Boyd household which included his son and sister-in-law also

---

[188] U.S. Federal Census for 1900 and 1880
[189] U.S. Federal Census for 1900, District 0012, Glasgow, Barren, Kentucky.
[190] U.S. Federal Census for 1900, District 0030, Owensboro, Daviess, Kentucky.
[191] U.S. Federal Census for 1900, District 0019, Rocky Hill, Barren, Kentucky.
[192] U.S. Federal Census for 1900, District 0027, Mining City, Butler, Kentucky.

reflects a 12-year old Cuban boarder named Amalia Mojena. There is no record of Boyd serving either though several Boyds were in the Third Kentucky.[193]

Cornelius and Mary E. Angel, age 45 and 50 respectively, hosted in their household a "grandson" born in Cuba named Enathiel Perry, age 14. A Cornelius Angel served as a Corporal in Company M, Third Kentucky in Cuba.[194]

Another Cuban child was Andra Ydeno, age 11 in 1900, living in Paradise, Muhlenberg County in the household of Samuel F. and Mary C. Knight. Their sons John O. Knight and Ellington L. Knight served in Company F, Third Kentucky.[195] There are other Cuban natives listed in the census but the connections to the Third Kentucky cannot be clearly made.

Members of Company F in Owensboro brought back 19-year-old Andrea Lopez. It was reported he had been a prisoner in Spanish lines and was 'adopted' by the company while in Cuba. He was to make his home with one of the officers.[196]

Among the other items brought back were gamecocks, specifically

> *"two pairs of Cuban Game fowls for Morrow & Crabb. They were purchased for them at Matanzas by Captain Logan Feland and were with the regiment until it was mustered out at Savannah, Ga. One pair are Genuine Cuban Blues and the other are Black breasted Red Games as bred in Cuba. They are*

---

[193] **U.S. Federal Census for 1900, District, 0016, Newport Ward 03, Campbell, Kentucky**
[194] **U.S. Federal Census for 1900, District 0084, Magisterial District 03, Lewis, Kentucky.**
[195] **U.S. Federal Census for 1900, District 0063, Paradise, Muhlenberg, Kentucky.**
[196] *Hickman (Ky) Courier*, May 26, 1899, 'Brought A Mascot'.

much smaller than the American games, the cocks weighing four pounds and the hens three pounds."[197]

Though the Red rooster had been in the fighting pits, the couples were to be used for breeding. Captain Feland would later become a Major General in the U.S. Marine Corps.

Another item brought back by George Thompson was a piece of a door from Moro Castle which he gave to his friend, Police Officer Zack T. Thomason who used the wood to make a billy club or nightstick.[198]

Not everything brought back was welcomed however. Will Hilton was discharged in Savannah and traveled to Rock Hill, South Carolina where he was to visit his brother. Smallpox appeared on his body and he was immediately isolated in a tent under guard to prevent the spread of the disease. He was cared for by a nurse who had previously contracted smallpox and was immune from infection.[199]

While many of the men returned to their pre-war careers, others became active in politics. On July 11, Lt. Col. Jouett Henry, now back in civilian status, accepted a call to become a Democrat candidate for the Christian County seat in the Kentucky General Assembly. He promised to "make an active and winning fight."[200] Against a field of four candidates, he tied in September 4 balloting by the Democrat

---

[197] *Hopkinsville Kentuckian*, May 19, 1899, 'Direct from Matanzas: Morrow & Crabb's Imported Cuban Game Fowls', page 5.
[198] *The Frankfort (y) Roundabout*, May 27, 1899, 'From Moro Castle', page 8. "Mr. Thomason's' son turned out a policeman's billy from the wood, and now Zack is as proud as a peacock of his new club."
[199] *Yorkville (SC) Enquirer*, May 27, 1899, 'Suspected Smallpox Case', page 2.
[200] *Hopkinsville Kentuckian*, July 11, 1899, 'For Representative: Two Democratic Candidates Already Announced', page 4 and 8.

committee. One vote changed and Henry lost out to a long-time party stalwart.[201]

Others still enjoyed the military life and made application for commissions in the new U.S. volunteer army being recruited for duty in the Philippines. Among the Third Kentucky Volunteers were Major Noel Gaines, to be attached to the 39th U.S. Volunteer Infantry as adjutant[202], Captain Burchfield,[203] Lieutenant Logan Feland,[204] Lieutenant James E. Rash,[205] First Lieutenant Robert E. Grinstead to serve with the 29th U.S. Volunteer Infantry[206], Captain Robert C. Payne with the 31st U.S. Volunteer Infantry, Lieutenant James R. Rash who was to serve as General Frederick Dent Grant's aide de camp and First Lieutenant and later Captain Arthur G. Sharpley, Quartermaster with the 31st U.S. Volunteer Infantry.[207],[208]

Sharpley, a son of Frankfort, Kentucky would end up in the 12th Cavalry. His career ended ingloriously on April 4, 1904 after a finding of guilt for "conduct unbecoming an officer and a gentleman in violation of the 61st Article of War." The charged centered on multiple specifications focused on

---

[201] He lost to D.R. Peery. See *Hopkinsville Kentuckian*, September 5, 1899, p1. 'Dennis R. Peery: Nominated for the Legislature by the Democrats'.
[202] U.S. Senate. 60th Congress, 1st Session. Document 441, Part 2. *Letter of the Secretary of War: List of Officers of Volunteers Organized Under Act of March 2, 1899, for Service in Philippines, Showing Travel Pay, etc.*
[203] *The Paducah Sun*, July 20, 1899 'News Notes'
[204] *Frankfort Roundabout*, July 15, 1899, 'Kentuckians Get There', page 7.
[205] *Evening Bulletin*, July 24, 1899, 'Lieutenant Carroll Power',
[206] Ibid, U.S. Senate Document 441.
[207] Ibid, U.S. Senate Document 441;
[208] *The Frankfort Roundabout*, April 27, 1901, 'Kentucky's Twelve' page 5; see also the Maysville, Ky *Evening Bulletin*, April 25, 1901, 'Lieutenant Carroll Power', page 2.

Sharpley's attempts to seduce the wife of one of his Sergeants while in Batangas Province in the fall of 1903.[209]

Heroes of Peace

While the men of the Third Kentucky Infantry did not share the combat fame of other units that served in the Spanish-American War, their service should not be dismissed as irrelevant.

The officers and non-commissioned officers of the Third Kentucky Infantry succeeded in bringing together a disparate group of volunteer companies to make what was generally viewed as a one of the best volunteer regiments in the Army.

While not in combat, they were not without casualties. And unlike many of their counterparts they were able to play a small role in humanitarian work and local security operations on a foreign shore. They enabled the return of peace and stability to a devastated Cuba. In this regard, they were heroes of peace. Their work foreshadowed in many respects, what would become standard missions for future generations of American veterans on foreign fields.

-finis-

---

[209] War Department. *General Orders and Circulars 1904.* (Washington: Government Printing Office) 1905. General Order No. 63, April 4, 1904. Finding of a General court-martial which convened at headquarters, Department of Luzon, Manila, Philippine Islands, pursuant to Special Orders No. 208, Department of Luzon, October 22, 1903; see also the Maysville, Ky. *Daily Public Ledger,* April 18, 1904, page 4 which reported, "First Lieutenant Arthur G. Sharpley of the Twelfth Cavalry, on duty in the Philippines, has been dismissed [from] the service for making love to the pretty wife of Sergeant Milton Heckert of his Regiment. Lieutenant Sharpley is a Frankfort man." Sharpley was transferred to the 12th Cavalry in October 1901 See *The Semi-Weekly Interior Journal,* October 4, 1901, page 4, 'News Notes' and *The (Washington) Times,* October 13, 1901, page 7.

Appendix 1

Chronological Record
of the
Spanish-American War
and the
Third Kentucky Infantry

1898

February 15	*USS MAINE* sunk in Havana Harbor
March 9	U.S. Congress passes bill to strengthen U.S. military.
March 28	U.S. Naval Court of Inquiry determines *USS MAINE* was sunk by a mine.
March 29	The U.S. government issues ultimatum to Spain to terminate its presence in Cuba.
April 1	Spain rejects the U.S. ultimatum regarding Cuba.
April 11	President McKinley requests authorization from Congress for U.S. intervention with the intent of ending the war between Cuban rebels and Spain.
April 13	Congress agrees to President McKinley's request but refuses to recognize Cuban rebel government.
	Spain declares the U.S. policy a threat to Spanish sovereignty and authorized monies for war.
April 19	Congress authorizes war with Spain (311 to

6 in the House and 42 to 35 in the Senate) specifically stating, thru the Senator Henry Moore Teller Amendment, that the U.S. did not intend to annex Cuba and would leave when the war was over and the island was pacified.

April 20 — President McKinley signs the Joint Resolution for war with Spain and notifies the government of Spain.

April 21 — The government of Spain recognizes the U.S. Joint Resolution as a declaration of war. All diplomatic relations are suspended. President McKinley orders a blockade of Cuba and Spain mines Guantanamo Bay.

April 22 — The U.S. blockade of Cuba begins.

April 23 — President McKinley calls for 125,000 volunteers to build an American Army to fight Spain.

April 24 — Spanish Admiral Cervera's fleet is dispatched from Cape Verde to Cuba and Puerto Rico.

April 25 — War is formally declared between Spain and the United States.

May 1 — The Battle of Manila Bay (Philippines). Commodore George Dewey destroys Spanish fleet.

May 6 — Kentucky Volunteers called out by Governor Bradley.

May 7 — Companies throughout the state start for Lexington.

May 8	State companies arrive at Camp Collier in Lexington.
May 12	American bombardment of Porto Rico, the first major battle of the Port Rico campaign.
May 21	Third Kentucky Infantry, U.S. Volunteers is mustered into the service of the United States with 46 officers and 945 enlisted men. The organization takes place over ten days.
May 25	U.S. Philippine Expeditionary Force (Eighth Army Corps) dispatched to the Philippines arriving in Cavite on 1 June.
June 1	Third Kentucky leaves Lexington for Chickamauga Park. Assigned to Third Brigade, First Division, First Army Corps.
June 2	Third Kentucky arrives at Chickamauga, being among the earliest of the volunteer regiments to reach the park.
June 10	U.S. Marines land at Guantanamo Bay, Cuba.
June 12	Philippine rebels under General Emilio Aguinaldo declare independence from Spain.
June 20	Guam surrendered to U.S. forces.
June 22	American forces under General William Rufus Shafter land at Daiquiri, Cuba.

June 24	Battle of Las Guasimas, Cuba.
July 1	Battles of El Caney and San Juan Heights in Cuba open access to Santiago.
July 3	Battle of Santiago Bay. The Spanish fleet is destroyed.
July 8	The U.S. annexes Hawaii.
July 17	Santiago surrenders to General Shafter.
July 18	Spain asks for a suspension of hostilities and begin to war ending negotiations via French intermediaries.
July 25	U.S. invasion of Porto Rico begins
July 26	France contacts the U.S. for Spain to request a suspension of hostilities.
July 27	Third Kentucky marches to Rossville, Georgia to embark on the cars for Newport News and thence to Porto Rico.
July 29	Third Kentucky arrives at Newport News expecting to take transports the next day for Porto Rico. Placed in camp.
July 30	The U.S. offers a counterproposal to Spanish request for a ceasefire.
August 1	Third Kentucky boards transport for Porto Rico. Once aboard, the order is countermanded and troops are sent back to camp.
August 2	Spain accepts the U.S. peace proposal for a

suspension of hostilities and negotiations

August 12	Spain signs armistice.
August 13	U.S. troops seize Manila.
August 16	Third Kentucky departs Newport News for Lexington.
August 17	Third Kentucky arrives in Lexington at midnight; assigned to First Brigade, Second Division, First Army Corps.
August 19	Third Kentucky arrives at Frankfort Pike Camp, on the Louisville Southern Railroad.
August 20	A detail from the Third Kentucky, under command of Captain Noel Gaines, is ordered to perform provost duty in the city of Lexington.
Sept 12	U.S. and Spanish officers meet in Havana to discuss evacuation of Spanish forces from Cuba.
Sept 13	The Spanish Parliament ratifies the Peace Protocol.
Sept 15	The Malolos Congress of the First Philippine Republic holds its first session.
Sept 17	Third Kentucky leaves Frankfort Pike camp and relocates to neighboring Camp Hamilton.
Oct 1	U.S. and Spanish peace commissioners meet in Paris for final negotiations for the Treaty of Peace.

Oct 25	President McKinley tells U.S. peace commissioners to insist on the U.S. annexation of the Philippines.
Oct 26	Pioneer detail under Captain Brinton B. Davis sent to Columbus, Georgia to prepare a winter camp for the regiment.
Nov 11	Third Kentucky departs Camp Hamilton, Kentucky and travels by L&N Railroad to Montgomery, Alabama by way of Nashville and Birmingham. At Montgomery regiment transfers to the Georgia and Alabama Railroad for trip to Columbus.
Nov 12	Third Kentucky stops at Bowling Green, home of Regimental Commander Colonel Smith. Three hour layover.
Nov 13	Third Kentucky arrives Columbus, Georgia on Sunday night, remaining in cars until Monday morning.
Nov 14	Third Kentucky marches from train station to camp.
Nov 29	The Philippine Revolutionary Congress approves a constitution for the Philippine Republic.
Dec 10	Treaty of Paris signed by U.S. and Spain. U.S. annexes Puerto Rico, Guam and the Philippines. Cuba becomes independent.
Dec 21	President McKinley issues the Benevolent Assimilation Proclamation but instructs U.S. forces in the Philippines to use force, as needed,

	to impose American sovereignty over the Philippines.
Dec 23	Guam placed under U.S. Navy control.

1899

January 1	Emilio Aguinaldo declared president of the Philippine Republic. The U.S. does not recognize the new government. All Spanish forces ordered out of Cuba.
January 17	Wake Island claimed by the U.S. for use as a cable link to the Philippines.
January 17	Third Kentucky leaves Columbus for Savannah en route Cuba.
January 18	Third Kentucky arrives in Savannah, boards ship and departs at 11 p.m. on board the transport *Minnewaska* (later renamed *USAT Thomas*). [210]
January 21	Third Kentucky arrives at Matanzas at 7 a.m.
January 27	Third Kentucky, Companies A, C, G and K assigned from Matanzas to La Union, Cuba.
January 30	Third Kentucky, Companies B, F, L and M assigned from Matanzas to Cardenas, Cuba.
February 4	The Philippine Insurrection begins.

---

[210] The *Correspondence* summary of the Third Kentucky, p595, names the ship as *Minnesota*. Public news records are clear the ship was the *Minnewaska*.

February 6	The U.S. Senate ratifies the Treaty of Peace (52 to 27).
March 3	Third Kentucky, Companies B, F, L, and M return to Matanzas.
March 19	The Queen regent of Spain, Maria Cristina, signs the Treaty of Paris. This action breaks a deadlock in the Spanish Parliament.
April 5	Companies A, C, G and K return to Matanzas.
April 7/8	Third Kentucky departs Cuba for Daufuskie Island, six miles from Savannah, Georgia. Companies A, C, G and K sailed on the *Florida*. Remainder of regiment sail on *Kilpatrick*.
April 10/11	Third Kentucky arrives at Daufuskie Island and remains in quarantine for one week.
April 11	The Treaty of Paris is proclaimed.
April 18	Third Kentucky leaves quarantine and encamps at Savannah.
May 16	Third Kentucky musters out of United States service in Savannah with 50 officers and 954 enlisted men. No officer casualties were incurred during the period. Seventeen enlisted men died of disease, two men were killed by accidents, one was murdered and 56 deserted.

Appendix 2

Division and Brigade Organization Third Kentucky Infantry

Organizationally the Third Kentucky Infantry was assigned to the First Army Corps The changing war requirements and rapidity of the conflict led to many reorganizations at the Division and Brigade level.

First Army Corps

May 31, 1898
First Division (MG James H. Wilson)
Third Brigade (Col. W. J. Hulings, 16th PA Infantry)

June 30, 1898
First Division (MG James H. Wilson)
Third Brigade (Col. W. J. Hulings, 16th PA Infantry)

July 31, 1898
First Division (MG James H. Wilson)
Third Brigade (BG Frederick Dent Grant, USV)

August 31, 1898
First Division (MG James H. Wilson)
Third Brigade (Col J.S.S. Culver, 5th Illinois Inf)

September 30, 1898
Third Division (BG Joseph P. Sanger, USV)
First Brigade (BG John A. Wiley, USV)

October 31, 1898
Second Division (MG William Ludlow, USV)
First Brigade (BG John A. Wiley, USV)

November 30, 1898
Second Division (MG William Ludlow, USV)
First Brigade (BG John A. Wiley, USV)

December 31, 1898
Second Division (BG John A. Wiley, USV)
First Brigade (Col. George W. Gunder, 160th Indiana)

January 16, 1899
Second Division (BG John A. Wiley, USV)
First Brigade (Col. Baldwin D. Spilman, 1st WV Inf)

Appendix 3

Regimental Roster

Third Kentucky Infantry
(1898-1899)

The Third Kentucky muster rolls contain multiple names for the same people reflecting over 1,915 names. Many of these were misspellings of the original name. These have been reviewed and corrected. In a case where it is uncertain a name reflects one person, both names are included. While extensive, the records do not reflect the names of other men credited by newspaper accounts as having served in the Third Kentucky. These have been added to the roster to ensure the record is as complete as possible giving 1,475 names.

The initial target strength for individual companies was 84 men with the wartime strength increased to 106 men. Many were discharged during the period of service. Company transfers, discharges and promotions created vacancies requiring new men. As a result, a company roster might have as few as 112 names or as many as 131 names. No companies are identified for 22 men, six are identified as non-commissioned staff and 17 are identified as 'field and staff'.

Abbreviations:
F&S = Field and Staff
NCS = Non-Commissioned Staff
QM = Quartermaster
Ranks reflect at time of enlistment/at time of discharge. If not designated, the rank is Private.

Name	Company	Rank
Abbott, John H.	L	
Abell, Joe C.	F	
Adams, John	G	
Adams, Samuel Q.	G	Corporal
Adamson, Walter P.	A	
Adkinson, Guy W.	M, C	
Albers, Herman	D	Musician/Private
Alderson, George B.	B	Corporal
Alexander, Lewis W.	F	Corporal
Algood, Aaron C.	F	
Allen, Bryant F.	I	
Allen, Edward F.	I	Wounded; accidental gunshot
Allen, James R.	K	Sergeant
Allen, Robert E.	F	
Allen, Robert L.	F	
Allen, William L.	H	
Allison, Harry F.	K	
Altmire, William H.	D	Sergeant
Alvey, William A.	H	
Anderson, George I.	F	
Anderson, John	L	
Anderson, Thomas	H	
Anderson, Trabue	E	
Andress, Harry	H	
Andrews, Isaac L.	I	
Andrews, Ollie N.	I	
Angel, Cornelius	M	Private/Corporal
Anglin, Moses	L	
Armitage, Arthur G.	E	

Armitage, James M	G	
Arnett, Alfred L.	D	
Arnold, Edward P.	D	
Arnold, Henry S.	I	
Arnold, James H.	I	
Arnold, John W.	A	Corporal
Arthur, Clarence A.	M	Sergeant
Ashby, Jesse A.	D	
Ashford, Alonzo C.	D	
Atkinson, Clarence Bryant	G	
Atkinson, Guy W.	C	
Atkinson, Hugh L.	H	Captain
Atkinson, Robert	C	
Atkinson, William T.	F&S	Assistant Surgeon/Captain
Aud, William E.	C	
Aultmire, William H.	D	Sergeant
Ausbrook, Robert P.	G	
Austin, Carl Harry	I	Sergeant
Autry, John F.	D	
Bailey, Alfred	L	
Baker, Basil	A	deserted 18 July 1898
Baker, Charles A.	K	
Baker, Hamilton W.	F	1st Lieutenant
Baker, Jacob	I	1st Sergeant
Baldwin, Frederick	M	Private/Wagoner
Baldwin, George T.	H	
Baldwin, Lee	C	1st Sergeant
Ball, Charles G.	G	Sergeant/Private
Ballard, Samuel H.	M	
Ballew, Arthur	K	Musician/Private

Banks, Melvin	M	Private/Corporal
Barker, Alva	B	
Barnes, Dudley B.	C	
Barnes, James C.	C	
Barnett, John J.	F	
Barrett, Robert L.	H	
Barrington, Frank J.	M	
Barry, Dave	E	
Bartholomew, Warren D.	D	
Barwald, George S.	K	
Basham, Arthur P.	F	
Basham, Claude H.	A	Private/Corporal
Bass, George E.	L	
Bates, George W.	K	Private/Artificer
Bauer, Christ	M	
Bays, Benjamin F.	M	
Beals, Robert H.	C	
Beam, John O.	C	Hospital Corps
Beard, Abby	C	
Beatty, John A.	K	Private/Musician (Band)
Beatty, Mart O.	K	Private (Band)
Bebout, Lewis L.	K	1st Sergeant/2nd Lieutenant
Beck, Charles T.	I	Private/Corporal
Beckett, Frank	B	
Beckham, David Y.	C	Captain
Beer, D.A.	G	
Beers, Louis H.	D	Hospital Corps
Bell, Albert	C	
Bell, Austin	F&S	Surgeon/Major
Bell, Charles G.	G	Sergeant/Private

Beller, Hezekiah J.	I	
Beller, Lonnie	I	
Bellew, Arthur	K	Musician/Private
Belomy, Doc	C	
Bemiss, Robert L.	C	
Bennett, Charley	G	
Bennett, Edward L.	D	Private/Corporal
Bennett, Estil	D	Private/Corporal
Bennett, Otis	D	
Bennett, R.	M	
Bennewitz, Theodore	I	
Benson, Clint	E	
Benson, George C.	I	
Benson, John H.	E	
Benson, Michael B	I	
Bentley, Isaac	L	
Berkley, Bertie	M	
Berry, Dave	E	
Bess, George E.	L	
Bickett, Frank L.	B	
Bilaine, W.S.	A	
Birk, Lewis N.	F	QM Sergeant
Bishop, George W.	M	
Bishop, Granville	L	
Bishop, Oscar	D	1st Lieutenant
Blair, Alexander	H	
Blair, John W.	M	
Blake, George M.	E	
Blake, Thomas	E	
Blakemore, Samuel T.	M	
Bligh/Blythe, Eli L.	M	
Bloomer, Walter C.	L	

Boatwright, Noble D.	K	
Bohlen, Henry	C	
Bohlen, Peter T.	C	Private/Corporal
Boles, Sydney L	G	Corporal/QM Sergeant
Boone, Albert	I	
Boswell, Henry F.	F	Private/Corporal
Bowe, Albert T.	C	Private/Musician (Band)
Bowe, Lebbeus L.	unk	
Boyd, Frank	F&S	Surgeon
Boyd, Frank	K, D	Corporal/Private
Boyd, Henry D.	F, B	
Boyd, John	G	
Boyd, Thomas	B	
Bozarth, Samuel J.T.	D	
Bracken, Samuel E.	D	
Bradley, Andrew J.	K	Private/Corporal
Bragg, Albert	A	deserted 8 October 1898
Brammer, Robert M.	M	
Brashars, John H.	I	
Bratton, George R.	E	
Brauner, Robert Lambert	E	
Breathitt, Gus	E	Corporal/Private
Breathitt, James M.	E	
Breathitt, Webber	E	
Brents, John M.	G	Private/Sergeant
Brewer, Allen W.	M	Captain
Brewer, Frank M.	M	Sergeant/1st Sergeant; died of typhoid fever.
Brewer, Thomas	M	Private/Wagoner

Brickey, June	D	
Brooks, Elmer L.	H	
Brooks, Henry Allen	H	
Brown, Charles W.	D	
Brown, Charles, L.	D	
Brown, Edward H.	E	
Brown, Ernest	E&A	Hospital Corps
Brown, George W.	M	
Brown, Henry C.	D	
Brown, Jay F.	M	
Brown, John M.	E	
Brown, Marion A.	G	
Brown, Thomas W.	C	Musician/Private
Brown, William H.	L	
Brown, William T.	C&G	
Bruce, Charles A.	C	Private/Corporal
Bruce, Waller C.	M	Private/Sergeant
Brumfield, Charles A.	E	
Brunner, Homer H.	H	
Bryan, F.W.	C	
Bryan, Frank M.	A	Private/Wagoner
Bryant, James C.	F&S	Major
Bryant, Jesse M.	K	
Bryant, Lex	K	
Bryant, Robert H.	H	
Bryant, Sylvester J.	D	
Bryant, Zach C.	K	
Buchanan, Edward	A	
Buchanan, John E.	E	Corporal
Buck, James E.	A	
Buckingham, Claude	L	Private/Corporal
Buckner, Robert H.	F&E	Musician/Private

Bullard, Gano	E	Sergeant
Bunch, Henry	L	
Bunch, John	L	
Bunch, Marion E.	I	QM Sergeant
Bunnell, Charles R.	C	
Bunnell, James H.	C	Private/Corporal
Burch, Earnest	F	
Burchell, Clay S.	E	
Burchfield, James A.	A	Captain
Burgess, James Robert	C	Private/Corporal
Burgess, Samuel	G	
Burnett, Joseph Flem	G	
Burns, Anthony	C	
Burns, Castle	M	
Burns, Edmund T.	E	
Burns, Joseph A.	G	
Burr, Virgil A.	G	
Burton, Whittinghill	D	
Bush, Henry	L	Private/Corporal
Bush, Robert H.	E	
Bush, Samuel R.	G	
Bush, Thomas C.	B	
Bushnell, Calvin A.	B	Private/Musician (Band)
Button, Peyton W.	M	Private/Corporal
Button, Servius T.	F	
Byrne, Joseph A.	G	
Caden, Ed	unk	Blacksmith
Cain, John	G	
Caldwell, Mike G.	K	Sergeant
Calvert, George	G	
Camden, Samuel M.	D	

Campbell, Andrew J.	E	
Canslor, James R.	A	
Caperton, Victor H.	L	
Cardin, Onley	M	
Carney, James	C	
Carr, Stephen D.	M	Hospital Corps
Carter, John C.	unk	
Carter, John E.	G	
Carter, Robert L.	I	
Cartwright, Charles J.	H	
Casazza, John P.	L	Private/Musician
Casey, Henry L.	E	1st Lieutenant
Castle, Cyrus H.	M	Artificer/Corporal
Castle, George Henry	L	
Castle, John	L	
Cates, Clayton L.	A	
Causey, Alonzo M.	B	
Cecil, Sylvester	F	Private/Corporal
Chamberlain, C.L.	unk	
Chandler, Jesse	M	
Chaney, Henry	L	
Chapman, Alex R.	F	Corporal
Chapman, Arthur G	F	Sergeant
Chapman, Louis P.	D	
Chappel, Frederick	B	
Cherry, Ariel C.	B, M & I	
Childers, Azro T.	I	
Childers, Henry	unk	
Chiles, Stratton S.	K	
Chilton, Isaac H.	L	
Chinn, Walter E.	L	Private/Corporal
Choate, Elbert L.	H	

Christian, Benjamin	C	
Christman, Edward L.	M	Private/Musician
Claggett, Robert H.	E	
Clark, Beverly L.	I	
Clark, Charles C.	C, D	Private/Artificer
Clark, Daniel T.	C	
Clark, Samuel	B	Captain
Clark,, George W.	H	
Clarke, Wade B.	F	
Clements, Thomas A.	F	
Clemmons, Edward J.	E	
Clere, Millard D.	D	
Cloud, James Stanley	C	
Cobb, Frank	E	
Cobb, Robert	F	
Cobb, William G.	H	Private/Musician
Cohan, William T.	F	
Cole, Ellie E.	I	
Cole, Estel V.	I	
Cole, George C.	L	
Coleman, Jacob D.	D	
Coleman, Milton J.	E	Sergeant
Coleman, Richard H.	K	
Coleman, Walter E.	K	
Collier, Benjamin F.	E	
Collins, Frank C.	L	
Collins, Herbert S.	B	
Collins, James L.	H	
Colson, David G.	F&S	Major
Compton, Robert Wood	G	
Conley, Dennis, B	M	
Conway, Millard	I	

Cook, David R.	K	Hospital Corps
Cook, Edward C.	A	died Ft. Monroe, 16 August 1898
Cook, Joseph W.	A	
Cook, William T.	I	Private/Corporal
Cooley, Richard	M	
Cooper, George M.	G	
Coots, Esker	I	
Coots, Jesse L.	I	Private/Corporal
Corey, J.J.	F	Sergeant
Corliss, Edwin M.	B&C	
Cornelius, William M.	E	Hospital Corps
Cornell, George J.	I	
Cornell, William J.	M	
Cosby, Harry T.	F	
Cothron, Francis E.	K	
Couch, Walter J.	E	
Courtney, Lafayette	E	
Cowles, Henry	B	
Cowles, Lonnie W.	B	
Cox, Clem	B	
Cox, Guy N.	H	Hospital Corps
Cox, Phin	B	
Crabtree, Anthony S. (Job)	I	
Crabtree, Carr	L	
Craig, Clyde V.	A	
Craig, Major	H	
Cramer, Louis A.	L	1st Sergeant
Crawford, James W.	L	Musician/Private
Craycraft, Lee	D	Sergeant/Private
Creekbaum, Angus	L	

Creekbaum, George W.	L	
Crews, John A.	H	
Crispin, Frank	K	Hospital Corps
Croal, John G.	K	Corporal/Sergeant
Crofut, Henry	L	
Crumbaugh, William I.	M	
Crump, John J.	I	Private/Corporal
Crutchfield, William C.	K	
Cundiff, Thomas	E	Hospital Corps
Cutsinger, Allen C.	A	
Dalton, John A.	G	Hospital Corps
Dalton, Lee	K	
Damron, William	unk	
Daniel, Lee J.	F	
Daubs, Edward A.	M	Private/Corporal
Davenport, Peter C.	I	
Davidson, Burnett C.	K	
Davidson, George C.	K	
Davies, Alfred	unk	
Davis, Brinton B.	K	Captain
Davis, Eldred A.	A	
Davis, Frederick H.	M	Corporal/Private
Davis, Jacob B.	K	
Davis, John L.	F	
Davis, John W.	M	1st Lieutenant
Davis, Nichols	C	
Davis, Pearl S.	A	
Davis, Shirley B.	A	
Davis, Ulysses S.	H	Corporal/Sergeant
Davis, William M.	A	
Davis, William P.	L	
Dawson, Peter Leo	C	Private/Band

Dawson, Robert E.	L	
Dawson, Steve B.	L	
Dawson, Wilbur	F	
Day, Alonzo	F	Private/Corporal
Day, George	L	
Dayton, John	L	
Dean, Harry L.	B	
Dean, Patrick B.	B	Corporal/Private
DeBord, Samuel J.	C	
DeBord, William M.	C	Private/Corporal
DeChamp, E. Beverly	K	Private/Corporal
Deckey, H.E.	K	
DeJarnett, George	H	
Delaney, Clifton	E	Wagoner/Private
Denham, John W.	B	
Denny, Frank	C	Private/Corporal
Denton, Henry	M	Killed in Columbus, Ga
Derman, James	I	
Diamond, M.G.	unk	
Diamond, Wayne F.	L	
Dicke, Henry E.	K	
Dickinson, Guy	G	
Dietrich, John R.	L	
Dillingham, Eugene	B	
Dillingham, Willie	F	
Dills, Edward	M	
Dinkelspiel, Ferdinand C. (Fred)	G	Private/Band
Dixon, James T.	C	
Dixon, Joseph K.	M	2nd Lieutenant
Dobbs, John H.	I	

Dodd, William A.	B	Private/Sergeant
Donahue, Joseph	D	
Donaldson, Harry G.	E	
Dorris, Dock	A	
Dorris, George W.	A	
Dorris, Guy Arthur	A	
Douns, Cortie L.	H	Wagoner
Dowis, Cager F.	L	Private/Corporal
Downard, Elmer O.	L	
Doyle, Emory C.	C	
Drake, Jay N.	L	
Drennan, Clay	D	
Dudley, Milton B.	H	
Duff, Edmund T.	G	Musician/2nd Lieutenant
Duke, Benjamin O.	B	Private/Corporal
Dunavan, Ned	B	Private/Corporal
Dunaway, Ernest	H	
Dunaway, James M.	H	
Duncan, Thomas W.	M	
Dunn, Arthur L	K	
Dupuy, Louis R.	F	
Durbin, Benedict	C	
Durham, Arid	C	
Durham, Joseph H.	I	
Duval, Claude C.	G	Sergeant
Dyer, James	unk	
Eadens, Grant D.	B	
Eatman, Eberly E.	G	
Ebert, Welbie	G	
Edginton, Harvey E.	C	
Edmunds, Charles P.	G	Private/Corporal

Edmunds, Chase	G	Private/Corporal
Edwards, Ira	C	
Egeman, William H.	C	
Ellegood, Edward	I	
Elmond, William E.	I	
Emberton, Samuel T.	A	
Embry, Jesse	I	
Englant, Samuel N.	L	
Ennis, Wallace W.	A	
Epperson, William C.	L	Private/Sergeant
Estep, James	L	
Evans, James M.	C	Private/Sergeant
Everett, William E.	G	
Ewing, Lee M.	B	Signal Corps
Fairchild, John A.	H	Corporal/Artificer
Farley, William H.	K	Corporal/Sergeant
Farmer, Allen C.	F	Private/Musician
Farris, Isaac N.	G	
Faulkner, Arthur W.	M	
Faulkner, Samuel	E	
Fauntleroy, Cap	K	
Favors, Jack A.	A	
Faxon, James A.	B	Private/Corporal
Feland, John	D	Captain
Feland, Logan	F	Captain/Corporal
Ferguson, Lewis W.	M	
Ferguson, William M.	A	
Ferree, Samuel	E	later in 31st USVI
Finley, Thomas E.	A	
Finn, James A.	C	
Fish, Egbert T	C	
Fish, James T.	C	

Fitzpatrick, William N.	G	
Fitzsimmons, Patrick	L	
Fleming, Lloyd	M	
Flesher, Thomas J.	B	Private/Artificer
Flewallen, Marion	I	
Floyd, Beauregard	L	
Follin, Squire H.	B	Private/Corporal
Forbes, Charles	L	
Ford, Harry H.	H	
Ford, Henry W.	H	
Ford, John H.	D	
Ford, Otis C.	F	
Ford, Richard P.	A	Wagoner/Private
Forgy, Monroe Perry	B	
Fortune, Charles,	D	
Foster, Dickie	G	Corporal
Foster, Taylor E.	G	
Frankey, John B.	H	
Franklin, Luther E.	A	
Frayser, George H.	F	1st Sergeant/Private
Frazier, Solomon B.	M	
Freeman, George F.	E	
Frogge, Garfield	K	
Fry, John B.	unk	
Fuller, Eben	I	Private/Musician
Fuller, William J.	H	Private/Musician
Fuqua, William H.	F	Sergeant/Private
Gaines, Dennis	I	Private/Corporal
Gaines, Noel	E	Captain
Galloway, Charles H.	I	Private/Corporal
Gamp, Harry	K	

Gans, Harry C.	F	Corporal
Gardner, Ransom J.	B	
Garner, Romelius M. (Shorty)	unk	Civilian Contractor; African-American
Garr, Hughes	H	
Garrard, Sam	A	Sergeant/QM Sergeant
Garrett, Nevil M.	F&S	Asst Surgeon/Captain
Garrett, Oscar	F	
Garrett, William	unk	
Garvin, Thomas	C	Musician/Private
Gaskins, Philip	D	
Gates, George U.	K	Private/Artificer
Gates, Hope	F	
Gatewood, Joseph L.	H	
Gavin, Thomas	C	Musician/Private
Gentry, W.P.	unk	
George, James H.	M	
George, William	M	
Gill, Joseph	L	
Gillem, Charles	D	
Gillen, James	I	
Gillispie, Richard M.	D	
Gipe, Samuel E.	F	Corporal
Girard, Harry L.	E	
Glass, Luke Q.	E	Private
Glenn, Clarence	F	
Glenn, Harris	F	
Goddard, George	K	
Gooch, Arthur	L	Artificer/Private
Goode, Chester D.	L	Corporal/Private

Goode, William J.	F	Private/Artificer
Gordon, Amos	G	Corporal/Sergeant
Gordon, B.	F&S	Sergeant Major
Gordon, Carey E.	F	
Gormley, John P.	L	
Gower, Walter	A	
Grady, Thomas	L	
Grady, William T.	F	Corporal/Sergeant
Grady/Greedy, Thomas	L	
Graham, Charlton M.	L	Corporal/Private
Graham, Thomas V.	I	
Graham, William H.	A	killed in Cuba; accidental gunshot wound, 31 Jan 1899
Grant, George A.	A	Private/Corporal
Graves, David Wilbur	F	
Graves, James R.	H	Sergeant/Hospital Corps
Gray, Archie S.	H	
Gray, Herbert S.	B	Corporal/Sergeant
Gray, Walter	K	
Greenwell, Joseph P.	C	Private/Corporal
Greer, Samuel W.	M	
Gregory, Theodore R.	M	
Griffin, Charles B.	H	Private/Corporal
Grigsby, Henry L.	C	Corporal
Grimes, Ethelbert G.	B	Private/Corporal
Grimes, Thomas E.	I	
Grinstead, Albert T.	G	
Groce, Joseph P.	B	
Grogan, James	K	
Grubbs, Virgil D.	B	

Grundy, W.E.	A	
Haas, Louis	I	Private/Musician
Haffey, William H.	K	
Hager, Edward D.	M	
Haggard, Leland	H	Private/Hospital Corps
Haley, Timothy	E	
Hall, Alonzo	M	
Hall, Claude B.	A	Private/Regimental Band
Hall, David	D	
Hall, Harry C.	F	
Hall, Lafayette	D	
Halsey, Anson, E.	D	
Hamilton, Ralph B.	L	
Hammonds, C.B.	F	
Hammons, William	D	
Hampton, John N.	M	
Hancock, Joseph M.	M	Private/Sergeant
Hancock, William T.	M	Private/2nd Lieutenant
Hankins, Albert	D	
Hankins, Thomas	A	
Hanks, Arthur	D	
Hanks, Charles	D	Private/Corporal
Harbert, Willie E.	F	
Hardin, William C.	F	Private/Corporal
Harding, Daniel H.	H	QM Sergeant
Harlan, Merril C.	A	Private/Artificer
Harlow, Emmett	G	
Harlow, Samuel Moss	G	
Harmon, John	H	
Harold, John S.	F	

Harper, Thomas R.	F	Sergeant
Harreld, Arthur C.	I	Sergeant/1st Sergeant
Harrell, James V.	B	
Harrell, Nick D.	B	
Harris, Benjamin D.	B	
Harris, Hensley G.	K	2nd Lieutenant
Hart, Leslie G.	K	
Harvey, Lum	B	Private/Corporal
Harvey, Marshall L.	L	
Hast, John C.	H	Private/Corporal
Hathaway, Lige	F&S	Officer's Contract Cook; African American
Hathorn, Melvin H.	H	
Havlin, Thomas A.	A	
Hawkins, John M.	A	
Hawkins, Robert	L	
Hawkins, Thomas	A	
Hawley, Frank J.	D	
Haws, James W.	I	
Hay, William V.	B	Corporal/Private
Haydon, John P.	C	Sergeant/Private
Hayes, Clarence B.	D	
Haynes, Willis M.	I	Private/Wagoner
Hays, Jack C.	K	
Hazelip, William W.	B	
Head, Herbert	F	
Helm, Herschel H.	I	Private/Corporal
Henderson, Garner W.	G	
Henderson, Hugh R.	F	
Henderson, Jesse T.	M	Corporal/Sergeant
Hendrick, Wilbur O.	B	Private/Corporal

Henry, Jouett	F&S	Lieutenant Colonel
Henry, William	F	
Herm, John	K	
Herr, John S.	F	
Hesse, Thomas	C	
Heston, Frank	L	
Hewlett, William B.	A	
Heyser, Roy O.	F	Private/Musician (NCS)
Hicks, George N.	H	
Hicks, Herschel	F	
Hicks, Roger	H	
Higdon, Wirt J.	F	
Higgins, Robert P.	F	Corporal/QM Sergeant
Hill, Alvin P.	I	
Hill, Brack	L	Corporal/Private
Hill, Frank, P.	K	
Hill, John F.	H	
Hill, John R.	B	
Hill, Rowland	B	
Hill, William R.	H	
Hilton, William D.	C	
Himes, Robert T.	C	
Hines, Arthur W.	F	
Hines, Frank G.	M	
Hines, Hiram M.	B	
Hines, James P.	M	
Hines, Warner W.	B	Private/Corporal
Hobdy, Charles L.	B	
Hobdy, Edward J.	B	Private/Corporal
Hobgood, Norman	A	

Hobson, James	B	
Hodge, Isaac S.	K	Private/Corporal
Hodges, Berry A.	F	
Hodges, Buron L.	B	
Hodgins, Berry A.	F	
Hodgins, George	D	
Hogarty, Michael A.	NCS	Chief Musician
Hohnstein, Moritz	M, L	
Holbrooke, James F.	L	
Holderman, William W.	F	Private/Corporal
Holland, William H.	B	
Holloway, Earnest	M	
Holman, William H.	G	Sergeant
Holt, Webb J.	unk	
Hoover, Noah W.	H	
Hope, Buel T.	I	Private/Musician
Hope, John A.	G	
Hope, William M.	I	
Hopkins, Henry H.	F	
Horn, T.	H	
Hoskins, Robert	E	
Houchin, Ward	B	
Howard, Charles B.	F	
Howard, J.	I	
Howard, Joseph R.	D	
Howard, Nathaniel T.	I	Captain
Howard, William	E	
Howell, Edward O.	F, B	
Howes, Harry C.	unk	
Hudnall, James A.	B	
Hudnall, James N.	I	
Hudson, Alfred L.	D	Private/Wagoner

Huff, Clarence C.	C	
Hughes, Bronner	G	
Hughes, Edward C.	F	Private/Musician
Hughes, James H.	M	
Hughes, William P.	L	
Hulsey, Ashel E.	D	
Hunt, Herman	I	Killed on return, accidental gunshot wound.
Hunt, Nitie E.	I	
Hunt, Ulysus G.	I	
Hurd, Clarence M.	B	
Hurst, John	C	Private/First Sergeant
Husk, Albert S.	B	
Hyman, Samuel	E	
Iglehart, Eben C.	A	
Iler, Quinton D.	D	
Ingram, Benjamin	L	
Ingram, Eli	L	Private/Corporal
Ingram, William H.	L	
Ireland, Craig	unk	
Ireland, Richmond	G	
Irvine, Samuel B.	C	Private/Wagoner
Irvine, Wilson	C	Private/Corporal
Irwin, Fletcher	G	Private/Corporal
Isnogal, Walter	I	Killed in train crash
Ivy, Frank	A	
Jackson, Charles E.	E	Corporal
Jackson, James F.	F-E-H	
Jackson, Ora	L	
Jackson, Robert	E	

Jackson, Thomas	K	Private/Sergeant
Jackson, Timothy C.	G	Private/Wagoner
James, James	A	died at Lexington, KY 21 Oct 1898
James, Thomas M.	M	Private/Corporal
Jenkins, Allen	B	Musician/2nd Lieutenant
Jenkins, Lee C.	L	
Jenkins, William H.	E	Private/Corporal
Jennings, James	A	
Jennings, Jeff	A	
Jewell, Snyder	H	Corporal/Private
Jockey, Joseph F.	D	Corporal/Private
Johns, Jesse B.	B	
Johns, John B.	unk	
Johns, Richard Emmett	B	
Johnson, Fred	A	
Johnson, Harry E	K	Private/Musician
Johnson, Hays	C	
Johnson, John R.	B	
Johnson, Robert A.	G	
Johnson, Stewart P.	H	Private/Corporal
Johnson, Thomas	D	
Johnson, Thomas A.	E	Private/Corporal
Johnstone, George M.	K	
Jones Walter, L.	M	Corporal/Sergeant
Jones, Amasa W.	B	
Jones, Ardy J.	A	
Jones, Charles	F	
Jones, Curtis L.	G	
Jones, Edmond	M	
Jones, Eugene	G	

Jones, Eugene T.	H	Artificer/Corporal
Jones, Harry	H	
Jones, Henry G.	A	
Jones, James W.	F	
Jones, John H.	H	
Jones, John W.	D	Private/Sergeant
Jones, Letcher H.	E	Private/Cook
Jones, Thomas J.	B	
Jones, Thomas M.	M	Private/Corporal
Jones, Walter L.	M	Corporal/Sergeant
Jouett, Henry	F&S	Lieutenant Colonel
Judd, John M.	I	
Kane, William F.	E	
Karnes, Ernest	K	Corporal/Sergeant
Keithley, John W.	K	
Kelley, Dink	M	Private/Artificer
Kelly, George	E	
Kelly, William	E	
Kemble, George W.	A	
Kendall, Harvey B.	A	
Kennedy, Daniel H.	E	
Kennedy, Walter F.	D	
Kenton, Evan	E	
Keown, Clarence A.	D	Private/Corporal
Keown, John G.	D	Captain
Kieffner, George W.	F	
Kilbreth, George P.	M	
Kilbreth, Joseph D.	D	
Kimble, Henry A.	unk	
Kincart, Luther N.	L	Corporal/Private; Signal Corps
Kindard, James A.	K	Killed in train

		crash
King, Edward J.	B	
King, Emery G	B	
King, Samuel L.	F	Corporal/Sergeant
Kinkaid, William	E	
Kissinger, Cleophus	I	
Kitchen, Alvie/Alva	H	
Knight, Ellington C.	I	
Knight, John O.	I	
Knipp, Charles W.	G	
Knox, Absalom	K	
Kohlhepp, Vance P.	G	
Kollenberg, Harry P	F	
Krause, Frederick	M	
Kuykendall, David	D	
Kyle, John W.	K	
La Master, Proctor L.	M	
Laffoon, Polk	A	QM Sergeant/Sergeant
Lainey, W.G.	M	
Lancaster, Charles E.	G	
Lancaster, Norvel E.	C	
LaRue, John C.	H	1st Sergeant/2nd Lieutenant
LaRue, Washington Irving	H	Corporal/Sergeant
Laswell, Beecher	F	
Lawrence, Claude	B	
Lawrence, Deward	L	Private/Corporal
Lawrence, William H.	L	Private/Corporal
Lawson, Victor Hugo	C	Sergeant
Laycock, Richard B.	A	

Layne, James B.	G	
Le Master, James F.	A	
Le Master, Proctor L.	M	
Leach, Richard L.	D	Private/Corporal
Lee, Alvin	I	
Lee, John	C	
Lee, William B.	L	Musician/Corporal
LeFevre, Charles V.	K	
Leibfried, George W.	F	
Lewis, E. Trigg	G	
Lewis, George R.	G	QM Sergeant
Lewis, James E.	H	Private/Wagoner
Lewis, Robert A.	B	
Lewis, William W.	D	Hospital Corps
Lightbody, William K.	C	
Linton, Ivoe	H	Private/Corporal
Linton, Renzo	H	
Lockett, William M., Jr.	H	Private/Corporal
Lofthouse, William R.	E	
Lofton, Edward	K	
Logsdon, Harrison H.	F	
Logston, William	G	
Long, Albert	G	
Long, Joseph L.	E	
Lovan, Silas F.	A	
Love, William	K	
Luckett, Hiram H.	D	
Lynn, John	E	
Madden, John T.	F	
Maher, Timothy J.	L	Private/Musician
Mahoney, Carter	I	

Mahoney, Flem	I	
Mahoney, John T.	M	
Mahoney, Luther	M	
Malin, Thomas R.	F	2nd Lieutenant
Maliwat, Hardin	L	Private/Wagoner
Mann, Charles W.	D	Private/Corporal
Mann, Horace K.	H	Private/Corporal
Martin, Charles C.	I	Private/Corporal
Martin, Hezekiah C.	I	
Martin, Ira A.	G	
Martin, Louis	B	
Martin, Marion	B	
Martin, Milton F.	NCS	Regimental Sergeant Major/QM Sergeant-Hospital Corps
Martin, Robert	G	
Martin, Walter N.	I	
Martin, William A.	C	
Martin, William M.	D	Private/Musician
Mason, Josph A.	H	Sergeant/Private
Massie, Joe	F	
Mathan, E	H	
Mathens, J.E.	H	
Matthews, Yetman	F	Private/Corporal
Matticks, Charles H.	unk	
Mattox, Lewis H.	I	
Mauly, Thomas	M	Musician/Private
Maupin, Thomas	L	
Maxey, Milburn A.	B	Musician
Maxwell, Nathan S.	B	Prviate/Wagoner
May, George R.	D	Corporal

May, Hiram	M	
May, Homer	F	
May, Marion	F	Sergeant/First Sergeant
May, Philip B.	F	
May, Samuel H.	M	
May, William	M	
Mayberry, Sherman	E	
McClain, James E.	H	
McClaud, Joseph	B	
McClelland, A.	C	Sergeant; severely beaten by mob of 12th NY infantry
McCloud, William I.	M	
McCord, John D.	A	Hospital Corps
McCormick, Theodore	C	
McCoy, Columbus N.	D	
McCoy, James	D	
McCoy, William G.	C	
McCue, ---		fatally stabbed in a crap game
McCulloch, Samuel H.	E	
McDaniel, Calvin O.	D	
McDaniel, George A.	B	
McDaniel, Robert F.	E	Private/Hospital Steward
McDonald, Henry L.	M	
McGill, James M.	C	Private/QM Sergeant
McGill, John R.	M	Private/Corporal
McGinnis, John T.	C	2nd Lt
McGinnis, Lewis	D	
McGowan, Robert	E	

McGrath, Frank W.	M	
McGuire, Henry P.	H	
McGuire, Lewis	D	
McHugh, William J.	H	Sergeant/Private
McIntyre, Harrison	C	
McKay, John	E	Private/Corporal
McKay, Lud	C	1st Lieutenant
McKinley, James B.	A	
McKnight, Fred S.	NCS	Musician/Horse Shoer
McLemore, Ernest A.	A	
Mclemore, Jesse D.	C	
McMannus, Robert	K	
McManus, James W.	H	Private/Hospital Corps
McMillan, John Thomas	G	
McMillon, Green	D	
McNally, John P.	C	
Meadow (or Meados), James T.	D,B	Corporal
Medley, Edward L.	F	
Medley, Harry/Henry M.	F	
Medley, William	F	
Meek (or Meeks), Millard F.	D	
Meek, Robert C.	unk	
Meissner, James A.	F	
Menah, Robert F.R.	C	Private/Musician
Menser, John M.	A	
Mercer, Ansel	D	
Meredith, Arthur L.	D	
Merritt, Marcus W.	K	
Middaugh, George C.	M	QM

		Sergeant/Sergeant
Milbern, Daniel R.	C	
Miles, Crossland E.	A	Hospital Corps
Millard, John A.	D	
Miller, Corbin	L	
Miller, George	K	
Miller, George	M	
Miller, George W.	C	
Miller, Harry	K	Hospital Corps
Miller, Joseph H.	I	
Miller, Robert	B	
Miller, Thomas	C	
Miller, William	M	
Miller, William H.	D	
Miller, William M.	C	
Milliken, Charles M.	B	QM Sergeant
Mills, George C.	E	
Mills, William C.	E	Private/Artificer
Milward, John B.	L	1st Lieutenant
Minton, Alex	A	
Mintyre, Harrison (Harry)	C	
Mitchell, Asher W.	B	1st Lieutenant
Mitchell, James	B	
Mitchell, Joseph D.	C, H	
Mitchell, Marshall A.	B	Corporal/Private
Mitchell, Robert C.	E	Private/Musician
Mitchell, Robert C.	H	
Mitchell, Robert S.	F&S	1st Lt/Regimental Adjutant
Mohler, James K	A	
Monarch, John W.	F	

Montgomery, Samuel	F	
Moonehand (or Moonichand), Henry P.	I	
Moore, Archie D.	I	Sergeant
Moore, Charles S.	E	
Moore, Jacob R. (John)	I	1st Lieutenant
Moore, John B.	L	Sergeant
Moore, Joseph H.	H	
Moore, Quinn	A	
Moorman, Henry D.H.	F	
Moran, John H.	E	
Morehan, Henry P.	I	
Morgan, Elijah W.	E	
Morgan, Erwin P.	E	
Morgan, Jesse S.	B	1st Sergeant
Morgan, Oda M	E	
Morgan, Peter R.	A	Private/Sergeant
Mormand, Newton	E	
Morris, Charles	D	
Morris, Richard	L	
Morrow, Thomas J.	B	
Morse, William H.	E	
Moss, Harlow Samuel	G	
Moss, Thomas O.	K	
Moss, Zelner	K	Private/Corporal
Mullen, Richard	C	
Munday, Thomas T.	L	Sergeant/Private
Munford, David B.	G	
Murphy, Albert E.	K	
Murphy, Aubrey E.	K	
Murphy, Robert L.	C	
Murray, James A.	K	Private/Corporal

Murray, Lloyd L.	H	
Murray, Patrick	C	
Murray, Robert E.L.	K	
Murry, E.	C	
Music, Grant	L	
Mussen, Jesse	F	
Myers, James W.	L	
Nall, Adrian	D	1st Sergeant/Musician
Napier, James K.	I	
Napier, William B.	I	Private/Corporal
Neel, Alven	F	Private/Wagoner
Neel, Temp	I	
Neighbors, James B.	B	
Neighbors, John L.	I	
Neill, Charles	I	
Neill, Thomas	C	Private/Band
Nelso, Bolling G.	unk	Sergeant Major
Nelson, Bolling G.	NCS	Sergeant Major
Nelson, Jack W.	K	
Nelson, R.S. (may be 'Jack W.')	K	
Nelson, William H.	D	
Neuman (or Hyman), Samuel	E	
Nightengale, Fred L.	A	
Nisbet, Ernest	A	1st Sergeant
Nisbet, Frank A.	A	Sergeant
Nisbet, Waller B.	A	
Nixon, John B.	F, E	Private/Sergeant
Norman, Benjamin H.	H	
Norris, Daniel B.	G	
Norris, Frank	F	

Nugent, Robert E.	B	Corporal/Sergeant
Nunn, John L.	A	
Nuttall, John P.	M	Sergeant
O'Beam, John O.	C	Hospital Corps
Oberdorfer, ---	I	
O'Brien, Edward T.	I, B	
O'Connell, William J.	M	
Offney, Henry C.	M	Corporal/Private
Oldfield, Joseph H.	D	
O'Neill, Frank J.	B	
O'Riley, Edward	C	
Orme, John L.	E	
Orr, William	I	
Osborne, James W.	C	
Overstreet, Everett	B	Sergeant
Owsley, Amos G	K	QM Sergeant
Owsley, George S.	K	Sergeant/Private
Pannell, Frank B.	D	Private/1st Sergeant
Parish, Ira	A	
Parke, Lester W.	K	
Parker, George	M	
Parker, Jack	F	
Parker, James Allen	M	
Parker, John B.	L	
Parker, Littleton	M	
Parker, Wallace	L	
Parrent, Mervin	E	Private/Corporal
Parson or Parsons, James M.	F	
Pate, Ernest H.	H	
Pate, John W.	H	

Name	Company	Rank
Pate, Robert	K	
Pate, Robert B. (or V.)	H	
Pate, William T.	F	
Patten, Frank J.	E	Corporal/Sergeant
Patton, James L.	D	QM Sergeant
Payne, Charles N.	F	
Payne, Robert	I	
Payne, Robert C.	E	2nd Lieutenant
Pearce, James A.	H	
Peck, ---	F	Sergeant
Pedigo, Henry C.	G	
Pedigo, John E.	G	
Pedigo, Tony L. (Larry)	G	
Pedigo, Walter	Band	Band/Private
Pedley, Ward P.	F	
Pence, Ira	C	
Pendleton, Polk	L	
Pendley, Elzie	I	
Pendley, Rumsey J.	I	Private/Sergeant
Pendley, William F.	I	
Perkins, Roy H.	L	
Perry, Charles C.	F	
Pettit, James R.	A	Sergeant
Phelan, Thomas R.	G	
Phillips, Harry S.	B	Corporal/Private; Hospital Corps
Phillips, John F.	D	Corporal/Private
Phillips, Joseph S.	B	
Phillips, W. Henry	C	
Pierce, Frank	F	
Pigg, Ulysses S. Grant	L	
Ping, Robert H.	C	

Pitman, Eli	D	
Pittman, Bert	F	
Pittman, George	H	
Pittman, Page	H	
Pittman, Sid	F	
Platt, William Thomas	H	
Plymale, Ballard P.	D	
Pollock, Lod	M	
Ponder, Willie	E	
Poole, Charlie S.	K	
Porter, Edward	E	
Porter, John C.	I	
Porter, Monsey	I	
Potter, Alvin C.	D	Private/Corporal
Potter, Edward R.	B	
Potter, June L.	A	Private/Corporal
Powers, Ott L.	A	Corporal/Sergeant
Powers, Walter	A	1st Lieutenant
Prentis, Ernest	F	
Presley, Wiley	C	
Preston, Flint	B	
Preston, Forest L.	M	
Preston, Frank M.	M	Private/Corporal
Preston, Frederick F.	M	
Preston, Lewis C.	L	
Preston, Morrell G.	M	
Preston, Paris F.	D, M	Private/QM Sergeant
Price, George T.	unk	
Price, Henry R.	G	
Price, Paul P.	A	2nd Lieutenant
Price, Walter	G	

Pritchett, Mike	A	
Pritchett, Orlean A.	A	
Prowse, Frank O.	E	
Puckett, John T.	L	
Pulliam, Ed	G	
Pulliam, Paul	B	Private/Corporal
Pulliam, Walter F.	E	
Purcell, William J.	C	
Pursley, Birt	B	
Pyles, Henry H.	D	
Quinn, John D.	E	
Rafferty, George	C	Lieutenant
Ragland, Ira	D	Private/Corporal
Railey, Fleming G.	G	Captain
Raines, Orlander J.	I	
Raisor, James	I	
Ramsey, Benjamin A.	A	
Ramsey, Miles W.	A	
Ramsey, Morton L.	K	
Rankin, William O.	H	Musician
Ranney, Charles R.	L	Private/Corporal
Ransom, William R.	B	
Rash, James R.	D	2nd Lieutenant
Ratliff, Edward	unk	
Read, Beverly G.	K	
Reading, William T., Jr.	E	
Reardon, William E.	C	
Redford, Frederick D.	G	Private/Sergeant
Redford, Harry	G	
Reed, John	B	
Reuter, Emil L.	L	
Reynolds, Charles M.	G	

Reynolds, Frank W.B.	L	Captain
Reynolds, Lewis P.	L	Private/QM Sergeant
Reynolds, Thomas L.	A	Private/Musician
Rhea, Stewart H.	K	
Rhodes, George K.	C	
Rice, Benjamin	A	
Rice, Jack T.	A	Private/Regimental Band
Rice, James A.	H	Hospital Corps
Rice, James J.	A	Private/Regimental Band
Rice, John W.	M	
Rice, Malcolm	L	
Rice, Nelson D.	L	Private/Band
Rich, George C.	G	
Richards, James L.	H	
Richardson, Hardy L.	G	Hospital Corps
Richardson, Larkin D.	K	
Riddle, William N.	C	
Riggs, Washington	M	
Riley, William D.	C	
Rives, Herbert E.	I	Hospital Corps
Rives, Rupert S.	I	Hospital Corps
Roark, Fred M.	H	
Roark, Larue T.	D	Private/Musician
Robb, Joseph W.	C	Private/Sergeant
Roberts, Lonnie	D	
Roberts, Samuel C.	D	
Robertson, James W.	K	Private/Wagoner
Robertson, Jasper Marion	I	
Robertson, John W.	L	Corporal

Robertson, Thomas H.	A	Private/Regimental Band
Robinson, David C.	L	
Robinson, Felix	E	Corporal
Robinson, Harlin R.	I	Private/Corporal
Rockhold, Frank	L	
Rogers, Arthur R.	G	Corporal
Rogers, George W.	H	Hospital Corps
Romans, John W.	D	
Rone, Buell	I	
Rone, Elwood	I	Private/Corporal
Rone, Tilden	I	Private/Corporal
Roy, Henry	E	Private/Corporal
Rucker, James H.	K	
Rudd, Emmett L.	K	
Rudy, William D.	K	Corporal
Ruegg, Robert	L	
Rule, Benjamin B.	M	Private/Corporal
Rule, Charles T.	M	Corporal
Runner, Charles B.	B	
Russ, Joseph R.	I	
Russell, George T.	G	
Russell, Jack M.	B	Sergeant
Ryan, Charles H.	F	
Ryan, Frank B.	B	Private/Sergeant
Ryan, Joseph M.	L	
Ryvers, David A.	H	
Sacks, Jacob	F	
Saffarrons, George C.	F&S	Major
Sales, Charles	H	
Sample, Oliver F.	F	
Sanders, Lillard D.	NCS	Hospital Steward

Sandidge, John, Jr.	G	1st Sergeant
Sasseen, Phelps, Jr.	H	Sergeant/1st Sergeant
Saus, William L.	B	Private/Musician
Sawyer, John H.	L	2nd Lieutenant
Scanland, James M.	H	
Scharz, Charles	K	
Schaven, John G.	K	
Scott, Clarence	H	
Scott, Harry	A	Private/Corporal
Scott, William	E	
Seaver, Albert J.	G	
Sebree, Richard L.	K	
Secrest, Harry R.	C	
Shacklett, Cecil P.	A	
Shadet, Frank L.	C, H	
Shanty, John N.	C	
Sharp, William A.	B, L	Sergeant
Sharpley, Arthur G.	F&S	3rd Battalion Adjutant/1st Lieutenant
Shaver, Alvey	A	
Shaw, Dennis D./George D.	E	
Shaw, Norman W.	G	
Shearer, William C.	K	Private/Corporal
Shelley, Lewis, W.	M	
Shelton, Sidney	C	
Sheriff, Ira	M	
Sheriff, Leslie	M	
Sherman, Henry B.	M	
Shifflett, James W.	B	
Shifflett, Thomas E.	G	

Shiplet, Robert	G	
Shirley, Luther H.	G	
Shive, Otis P.	G	Private/Principle Musician
Shoemaker, Thomas J., Jr.	H	
Simcox, Joseph S.	F&S	1st Battalion Adjutant/1st Lieutenant
Simmons, Shelby	B	
Simmons, Walter A.	B	
Simpson, Beverly A.	D	
Sinclair, Charles B.	I	
Singe, Jacob	H	
Sinnett, Joseph T.	K	
Sisk, Silas H.	A	
Skaggs, William L.	B	
Slater, Edward S.	M	Private/Corporal
Slaton, Charles A.	H	Private/Corporal
Slatten, James E.	D	
Sleet, Harry	A	Private/Corporal
Slinker, James Ernest	G	
Sloan, Till	G	
Smart, Virgil E.	B	
Smith, Alvin	E	
Smith, David H.	A	
Smith, George C	B	Private/Hospital Corps
Smith, George Lancaster	C	Private/Corporal
Smith, Henry E.	D	
Smith, John L.	G	
Smith, Joseph H.	K	
Smith, Leslie	F	

Smith, Mack	A	
Smith, Paul P.	F	
Smith, Robert H.	C	
Smith, Seaborn G.	B	Private/Corporal
Smith, Thomas J.	F&S	Colonel
Smith, William H.	A	
Snell, Getty E.	F&S	2nd Battalion Adjutant/1st Lieutenant
Snider (or Snyder), Rufus H.	C	Private/Corporal
South, Samuel F.	H	1st Lt
Spann, Thomas L.	G	
Sparks, James T.	M	
Spaulding, Samuel E.	H	
Spears, George	L	Private/Corporal
Speckman, Henry F.	D	Corporal
Spencer, John D.	G	
Spiceland, Jesse H.	D	
Spicer, James A.	L, F	Corporal/Private
Spradlin, Benjamin J.	M	
Sprague, John L.	I	
Spring, Joseph F.	L	
Sproule, John F.	I	Died of brain concussion.
Spurlock, Harry D.	C	Private/Musician
Stahl, Fred O.	C, L	
Stallard, Marvin	E	
Stanley, Clarence H.	D	
Stanley, George W.	G	Corporal
Stanton, Stoddard J.	E	
Stark, Charley T.H.M.	G	
Starling, Edward W.	E	Sergeant

Name	Co.	Rank
Starret, J.C.		Contract Teamster
Stater, Samuel E.T.	B	
Statton, Jesse S.	L	Corporal
Steele, William	E	
Steffee, Joseph	E	
Sterling, George A.	G	
Stevens, Edward A.	K	Private/Corporal
Stevens, Henry	L	Sergeant/Artificer
Stevens, Thomas J.	D	
Stewart, Alfred D.	K	1st Lieutenant
Stewart, Joseph A.	D	
Stewart, Thomas W.	A	Artificer/Private
Stewart, William P.	A	
Stier, William E.	K	
Stigers, Curt	E	
Stiles, Edward L.	D	Corporal/Private
Stites, John	E	
Stivers, McCreary	M	
Stocker, John J.	C	
Stokes, Virgil P.	A	
Stone, Robert P.	D	
Stone, Stanton	D	Wagoner
Stout, James J.	G	Corporal
Stout, Preston A.	G	
Stovall, Elbridge	B	
Strange, Frank L.	F&S	Quartermaster/1st Lieutenant
Strange, Hannibal H.	G	
Straunty, John N.	C	Private/Corporal
Stringer, William M.	A	
Stuart, John W.	C	Private/QM Sergeant

Sullivan, William N.	C	
Sutton, John W.	L	
Sutton, William H.	G	Private/Corporal
Sweatt, John W.	A	
Sweeney, James Henry	H	Private/Corporal
Sweeney, John N.	I	2nd Lieutenant
Sweeney, Lee	L	Wagoner/Private
Sweets, Edward C.	F	
Szymanski, August	E	
Taber, William H.	K, H	
Tackett, Charles S.	M	
Talbert, Mitchell	M	Private/Musician
Talbott, John Daniel	C	
Tansill, Charles A.	H	Private/Sergeant
Tayler, Clarence T.	G	Private/Musician
Taylor, Adolph	G	
Taylor, Frank	H, L	
Taylor, James	A	
Taylor, James C	G	Private/Musician
Taylor, Leland W.	H	
Taylor, Miner H.	M	
Taylor, Thomas W.	A	
Taylor, William E.	L	Private/Sergeant
Theisen, Frank J.	K	
Thomas, Frank M.	F&S	Chaplain/Captain
Thomas, Hiram P.	E	1st Sergeant
Thomas, Marion A.	E	Private/Wagoner
Thompson, Edward S.	C	
Thompson, George T.	E	
Thompson, Hugh G.	E	Private/Corporal
Thompson, Mitchell R.	M	1st Sergeant/2nd Lieutenant

Thompson, Vertner M.	L	
Thompson, William T.	B	
Thornberry, Marvin	F	
Thurman, Will	K	
Tilley, George W.E.	K	
Townsend, Elmo	K	
Townsend, Swain	K	Private/Corporal
Trigg, Haiden B.	G	
Trigg, Rice Ballard	G	1st Lieutenant
Trigg, Thomas H.	G	
Trotter, Cecil	K	Hospital Corps
Trout, Ralph B.	D	
Trueman, Chapman	B, NCS	Private/QM Sergeant
Tullis, William J.	H	
Turner, George W.	E	
Turpin, Steve D.	F	
Tutt, George D.	A	Corporal/Sergeant
Twohig, William J.	C	Private/Corporal
Tygart, Vincent E.	M	
Ullman, Jesse	K	Private/Corporal
Underwood, Pink W.	K	
Utley, Aspasia	A	
Van Hoose, Alonzo F.	M	
Van Hoose, George W.	M	
Van Hoose, James	M	
Van Hoose, Verner V.	M	
Vance, Sidney	M	
Vance, William M.	unk	
Vanhoose, Clyde	C	
Vanhoose, Herbert H.	C	
Vaughan, Benjamin Z	G	

Vaughn, Otho	E	Private/Corporal
Vickory, Joseph Lewis	G	
Vinson, Jay A.	M	Corporal/2ndLieutenant
Vittitoe, Charles C.	C	
Wade, Hall	unk	
Wade, James W.	D	Sergeant/QM Sergeant
Waggoner, Samuel T.	C	Private/Artificer
Walford, George F.	D	Private/Corporal
Walker, Harry W.	L	
Walker, Samuel	K	
Wallace, Ernest T.	K	
Waller, Charles S. (also E.)	E	Corporal
Wallingford, William R.	A	
Walp, Rupus	F	Private/Corporal
Walters, Clarence	L	
Walters, Flavins	K	
Walton, Oscar	A	
Ward, Bishop	H, E	
Ward, Eugene	G, I	
Ward, James Kent	I	Private/Corporal
Ward, John H.	M	
Ward/Wood, Elrod	G	
Ware, Ross P.	K	Corporal/Sergeant
Warren, Lewis T.	H	
Warrick, Earl C.	K	Corporal
Wathan, Joseph Eugene	H	
Wathen, George A.	H	
Wathen, W.H.	H	
Watson, B. (poss Bradley Wilson)	A	Sergeant

Watson, Dillie G.	A	Corporal
Watson, John E.	B	
Watt, Edward H.	F&S	Major
Watts, John W.	K	
Watts, W.W.	A	
Webber, Hilton F.	B	Corporal/Cook
Wedding, Charles L.	D	
Weil, Herman B.	K	Corporal
Weiner, Max	H	
Welch, Arthur	B	
Welch, Lamar	F	Corporal/QM Sergeant
Wells, Thomas S	H	
Wertheimer, Buford T.	H	Private/Corporal
West, D.J./James	G	
West, R.C.	D	Sergeant
Westmoreland, Millard T. (also W.)	D	Sergeant/Corporal
Westray, Thomas L.	G	
Whallen/Whalen, Filen	B	
Wheeler, Harry C.	K	Sergeant/Private
Wheeler, Herbert C.	M	Private/Sergeant
Wheeler, John W.	L	Corporal/Private
Whitaker, Calvin Vallie	I	Musician/Private
Whitaker, Thurman L.	I	
White, Lonnie F.	B	
White, Richard B.	B	
White, Robert J.	G	Sergeant/QM Sergeant
Whitehead, Edward A.	H	
Whittaker, Thomas/Thurman	I	
Whittinghill, Burton	D	

Wickliffe, Charles H.	L	QM Sergeant/Private
Wicks, James M. (also H.)	E	QM Sergeant
Wigginton, Julian K	C	Private/Hospital Corps
Wilhelm, John M.	H	
Wilhelm, Robert S.	K	Sergeant/Sergeant Major
Wilhoyte, John	F	Private/Corporal
Wilkes, Robert	E	
Wilkins, John M.	B	Sergeant/Private
Wilkins, Larkin B.	B	
Wilkinson (or Wilkerson) John B.	G	Private/Artificer
Wilks, Edgar W.	E	
Wilks, Robert	E	
Williams, Aubie/Antie	B	
Williams, Ed	K	
Williams, Emit	G	
Williams, Frank C.	M	Private/Corporal
Williams, Henry C.	B, M	Private/Musician
Williams, James R.	B	
Williams, Owen G.	D	
Williams, Thomas	D	
Williams, Thomas J.	E	
Williams, William E.	K	
Williams, William S.	L	
Williamson, Sanford	B	
Willis/Welbie, Ebert	G	
Willoughby, Charles H.	B	Private/Corporal
Wilson, Bradley	A	Sergeant/Private
Wilson, Edgar E.	K	

Wilson, Given P.	A	Corporal
Wilson, James W.	C	
Wilson, John J.	H	
Wilson, Joseph W.	C	
Wilson, Lewis,	C	
Wilson, Robert H.	E	
Wilton, William H.	C, G	
Wilton, William M.	G	
Wilton, William W.	C	
Winchel, James	B	
Winchell, Dow W.	B	
Windburn, Gus	I	
Winfree, William B.	E	Musician/Private
Winfree/Winfrey, Albert	K	
Wings, Walter W.	A	
Winn, George P.	M	
Winn, George William	M	
Winscott, Alfred	C	
Winters, Otis T.	C	
Withers, Milton Hunt	H	
Witherspoon, Elmer E.	A	
Witty, William B.	A	
Wolfe, Elijah K.	D	Private/Corporal
Wood, James W.	H	
Wood, John W.	H	
Wood, Joseph B.	G, B	Corporal/Private
Woodford, C.E.	A	
Woodward, Benjamin S.	L	Corporal
Wooldridge, Oscar	I	
Woolfork (or Woolfolk), Carl E.	A	Corporal
Wooten, Eugene A.	G	

Wootton, James M.	E	Artificer/Private
Worick, Earl C.	K	Corporal
Worner, John W.	A	
Worthingotn, William M.	A	
Worthington, Seth B.	F	
Wright, Frank H.	G	USV Signal Corps
Wright, Garland Jack	A	
Wright, George W.	L	
Wright, James W.	A	
Wright, Wilson T.	F	
Wyatt, George R.	E	Private/Musician
Yates, Matison	F	
Yates, William W.	A	
Yeaman, James M.	K	Corporal/2nd Lt.
Yelton, Alonzo	I	
York, George D.	D	Sergeant
Young, Champ C.	L	Corporal
Young, John L. (or S.)	C	
Young, William J.	K	
Yount, John	C	
Zimmer, Elon P.	E	Sergeant
Zufall, Max	M	

Bibliography

Primary Sources

Barnes, Horace F. *The Cuban Industrial Relief Fund'*. Article in Education, A Monthly Magazine Devoted to the Science, Art, Philosophy and Literature of Education. Volume 19 (September 1898-June 1899), p369. (Boston: Kasson & Palmer) 1899   Horace F. Barnes was the Financial Director of the Boston based Cuban Industrial Relief Fund.

Castleman, John B. Active Service (Louisville, Ky: Courier-Journal Job Printing Company, Publishers) 1917.

Kentucky. General Assembly. Senate. Journal of the Regular Session of the Senate of the Commonwealth of Kentucky (Louisville, Ky: The George G. Fetter Printing Company) 1902.

---. Acts of the General Assembly of the Commonwealth of Kentucky Passed (Louisville, Ky: George G. Fetter Printing Company) 1901

New York. Adjutant General. New York in the Spanish-American War 1898. Part of the Report of the Adjutant-General of the State for 1900. In Three Volumes. Volume II. (Albany: James H. Lyon, State Printer) 1900.

Taylor, William Thomas. The William Thomas Taylor Papers: Company A, Third Kentucky U.S. Volunteer Infantry. Edited by Greg Eanes. (Crewe, Va: The Eanes Group, LLC) 2015

Unknown. Photographic History of the Spanish-American War: A Pictorial and Descriptive Record of Events on Land and Sea with Portraits and Biographies of Leaders on Both Sides. (New York: Pearson Co.) 1898

United States of America, Bureau of the Census. *Tenth Census of the United States, 1880* and *Twelfth Census of the United States, 1900*. Washington, D.C.: National Archives and Records Administration, 1900. T9 and T623 respectively, 1,454 and 1,854 rolls, respectively.

Congress. Report on the Origins and Spread of Typhoid Fever in U.S. Military Camps during the Spanish War of 1898 (Washington: Government Printing Office) 1904. Document No. 757, 58th Congress, Second Session.

Congress. Report of the Commission Appointed By the President To Investigate the Conduct of the War Department in the War with Spain, 8 Volumes, (Washington: Government Printing Officer) 1900. Document 221. 56th Congress, 1st Session.

---. Correspondence Relating to The War With Spain and Conditions Growing Out of the Same Including the Insurrection in the Philippine Islands, in two Volumes (Washington: Government Printing Office) 1902

---. National Archives Records Administration (NARA). Spanish-American War Service Record Index. Alphabetical card index to the compiled service records of volunteer soldiers in the Spanish-American War, arranged alphabetically by state or territory. Publication Number M871. Record Group 94. Accessed through FOLD3 subscription data base.

---. Report of the Commission Appointed by the President to Investigate the Conduct of the War Department in the War with Spain. (Washington: The Government Printing Office) 1899

---. Senate. 60th Congress, 1st Session. Document 441, Part 2. *Letter of the Secretary of War: List of Officers of Volunteers Organized Under Act of March 2, 1899, for Service in Philippines, Showing Travel Pay, etc.*

War Department. United States. Annual Report of the Secretary of War. *Report of the Chief of Engineers, Part 1* (Washington: Government Printing Office) 1901.

---. *General Orders and Circulars 1904.* (Washington: Government Printing Office) 1905.

---. *Letter of the Secretary of War Submitting A Consolidated Statement of Fiscal Affairs In the Island of Cuba, Under the United States Military Government, from January 1, 1899 to April 30, 1900.* To U.S. Senate Committee on Relations with Cuba. As Audited. Division of Customs and Insular Affairs. December 13, 1900. (Washington, DC: Government Printing Office) 1900.

---. *Report of General James H. Wilson to the Adjutant General of the Army, 14 August 1899, Headquarters Department of Matanzas.* Contained in the Annual Report of Brigadier General James H. Wilson, U.S.V., Commanding the Department of Matanzas and Santa Clara to Which Is Appended Special Report on the Industrial, Economic and Social Conditions Existing in the Department at the Date of American Occupation, and at the Present Time. Matanzas, Cuba, August 1st – September 7th, 1899.

Unknown. 'The Cuban Industrial Relief Fund', page 247. Article in New Outlook, Volume 64, February 3, 1900.

Wilson, James Harrison. Under the Old Flag: Recollections of Military Operations in the War for the Union, the Spanish War, The Boxer Rebellion, etc. Volume II, (New York: D. Appleton and Company) 1912.

Secondary Sources
Bettez, David J. Kentucky Marine: Major General Logan Feland and the Making of the Modern USMC. (Lexington:

University of Kentucky Press) 2014.

Cosmas, Graham A. 'Securing the Fruits of Victory: The U.S. Army Occupies Cuba, 1898-1899'. Military Affairs, Volume 38 Issue 3 (October 1, 1974) p85-91. *Society for Military History Full Text Collection*, EBSCOhost (accessed April 18, 2016).

Tone, John Lawrence. War and Genocide in Cuba, 1895-1898. (Chapel Hill, NC: University of North Carolina Press) 2008.

Womack, Todd. *"Spanish-American War in Georgia."* New Georgia Encyclopedia. 22 October 2015. Web. 30 March 2016.

Newspapers (Kentucky)
The (Earlington, Ky) Bee
The (Paris, Ky) Bourbon News
The Breckenridge News
The (Marion, KY) Crittenden Press
The (Hopkinsville) Daily Kentuckian
Daily Public Ledger (Maysville, Ky)
The (Lancaster, Ky) Central Record
The (Maysville, Kentucky) Evening Bulletin
The Frankfort (Ky) Roundabout
Hartford (Ky) Herald
Hartford (Ky) Republican
The Hickman Courier
The Hopkinsville Kentuckian
Owingsville (Kentucky) Outlook
Paducah Daily Sun
The Richmond (Ky) Climax
The Spout Spring (Ky) Times
The (Stanford, Ky) Semi-Weekly Interior Journal

Newspapers (Other States)
Accomac (Va) Peninsula

Barre (Vermont) Evening Telegram
The Brooklyn (New York) Daily Eagle
The Columbus (Neb) Journal, April 19, 1899
The Copper Country (Illinois) Evening News
The (Washington) Evening Star
Graham (Arizona) Guardian
Herald (Leadville, Colorado) Democrat
The (Los Angeles) Herald
Houston Daily Post
Jamestown (North Dakota) Weekly Alert
The Kansas City Journal
Marietta (Ohio) Daily Leader
New York Daily Tribune
The (Sacramento) Record-Union
The (New York) Sun
Omaha Daily Bee
Richmond (Va) Times Dispatch
Rock Island (Illinois) Argus
The Salt Lake Herald
The Scranton Tribune
The Seattle Post-Intelligencer
The (Washington) Times
The Topeka (KS) State Journal
The True (Paw Paw, Michigan) Northerner
The San Francisco Call
Wheeling (West Virginia) Daily Intelligencer
The Wichita Daily Eagle
Yorkville (SC) Enquirer

Websites
Find A Grave
Bowling Green Kentucky (https://archive.bgky.org)
Lexington Museum of History (http://lexhistory.org)

ABOUT THE AUTHOR

Greg Eanes of Crewe, Virginia is a journalist, businessman, freelance writer and educator. He retired as an Air Force Colonel in August 2011 after 34 and one-half years uniformed service that included 23 and one-half years active duty. He supported intelligence operations during the Cold War, the Iranian Hostage Crisis, Operations DESERT SHIELD and DESERT STORM where he was the Evasion and Escape Intelligence Officer and acting Chief of Targets for Special Operations Command-Central; Operation IRAQI FREEDOM with two tours leading the Scott Speicher Investigation for the Iraq Survey Group and Operation ENDURING FREEDOM where he served as the Deputy and Acting Chief of Human and Counterintelligence for Combined Forces Command Afghanistan. He holds the Bronze Star Medal with an Oak Leaf Cluster for meritorious wartime achievement and various other wartime decorations..

Between 1993 and 2002 he held several community and elected positions to include Crewe Town Council and the Nottoway County School Board. He has a Master's Degree in Military History from American Military University and a Bachelor's Degree from Southern Illinois University-Carbondale. He has been certified by the Virginia Courts System as an expert witness in military history and veterans affairs. He speaks extensively on military history related topics particularly as they pertain to Virginia He has published multiple works. His books can be accessed through local libraries and bookstores.

He is married to the former Rosanne Lukoskie of Shamokin, Pennsylvania. They have two adult daughters, Amelia J. Eanes and Amanda Eanes Reed, a son-in-law Donald Aaron Reed and two grandsons, Jase and Avery Reed.